ACROSS CANADA TO THE KLONDYKE

Across Canada to the Klondyke

Being the Journal of a Ten Thousand Mile Tour
through the "Great North West," July 19th – October 13th, 1900

by

"Col. D. Streamer"
(Harry Graham)

Edited and with an introduction
by Frances Bowles

Ⓜ METHUEN

Toronto   New York   London   Sydney   Auckland

Captain Graham's Journal
Copyright © 1984 by Virginia Thesiger

Introduction
Copyright © 1984 by Frances Bowles

All rights reserved. No part of this publication may be
reproduced, stored in a retrieval system or transmitted
in any form or by any means, electronic, mechanical,
photocopying, recording or otherwise, without the
prior written permission of Methuen Publications,
2330 Midland Avenue, Agincourt, Ontario,
Canada, M1S 1P7.

Canadian Cataloguing in Publication Data
Graham, Harry, 1874–1936
    Across Canada to the Klondyke

Bibliography: p. 175
ISBN 0-458-98240-7

1. Northwest, Canadian—Description and travel—
1870–1905. * I. Bowles, Frances. II. Title.
FC3205.3.G73 1984   917.1'0456   c84-098836-2
F1060.9.G73 1984

Design: The Dragon's Eye Press
Maps: Geoffrey Thomson

Printed and bound in the United States
1 2 3 4 5 84 89 88 87 86 85

Contents

Acknowledgments

I appreciate the courtesy and cooperation I have received from
many people, and would like particularly to thank the following:

Mrs. Virginia Thesiger, of London, England, for permission
to publish her father's Journal, on which she holds the copyright. Mrs. Thesiger has been most generous in discussing the
project with me and in giving me information about her father.

The Trustees of the National Library of Scotland, Edinburgh, which owns the original typescript of the Journal,
kindly assented to its publication and to the use of quotations
from the Minto papers in the National Library's collection.

The current Lord Minto, who agreed to the use of quotations from family papers.

I am also grateful to Mr. James S. Ritchie, Keeper, Department of Manuscripts, National Library of Scotland (now retired), whose assistance and cooperation have been invaluable.

My sincere thanks also go to the Public Archives of Canada,
the Provincial Archives of Manitoba, the Provincial Archives of
British Columbia, Kenora Public Library, British Museum
Newspaper Library and the Library of the University of Winnipeg.

Introduction

"I think if Mary will allow me, I will send you home Harry Graham's journal, which is a wonderful work he has presented us with and will tell you every detail." So wrote Lord Minto, Governor General of Canada, to Arthur Elliot, his brother in Scotland, November 25, 1900.

Captain Harry Graham of the Coldstream Guards (hence the pseudonym "Col. D. Streamer") had accompanied His Excellency and Lady Minto on a 10,000-mile tour across Canada and north to Dawson City as an Aide-de-Camp to the Governor General and also as Acting Military Secretary. His account of the journey, which he presented to the viceregal couple, remained in the possession of the Minto family until the National Library of Scotland acquired the Minto papers in 1958.

The study of history is dependent on the diary keepers, journalists and record keepers of the times. Most often, such primary sources are dull reading, skimpy of fact and skimpier of anecdote, but occasionally a writer of both wit and ability will make a record of events significant to the shaping of a nation. When such a record survives, posterity is gifted with history which achieves a delicious blend of information and readability.

Harry Graham was such a writer. His journal, *Across Canada to the Klondyke*, by its recording of the contemporary scene and its humour, foreshadowed the highly successful career which he was to enjoy as an author of prose, humorous verse, play adaptations, librettos and lyrics for musical comedy.

Harry Jocelyn Clive Graham was born in London on December 23, 1874, the second son of Sir Henry John Lowndes Gra-

ham, KCB, and his first wife Lady Edith Elizabeth Gathorne-
Hardy, daughter of the Earl of Cranbrook. His father was a
Barrister of the Inner Temple who became Clerk of Parlia-
ments and as such resided at Royal Court, Palace of Westminster. His elder brother, Sir Ronald Graham, served with
the British Foreign Office and in 1921 was appointed British
Ambassador in Rome.

Educated at Eton and Sandhurst, Harry Graham joined his
regiment, the Coldstream Guards, in 1895 and was appointed
ADC to Lord Minto in 1898. He sailed to Canada with the
couple, their family and staff, arriving at Quebec on November
12, 1898. Here they were met by Lord Aberdeen, the retiring
Governor General, and here the Earl of Minto was sworn in as
the eighth Governor General of the Dominion of Canada.

Captain Graham served as ADC from 1898 to 1901 and again
from 1903 to 1904. When his original appointment expired in
the fall of 1901, he immediately proceeded to South Africa on
active service. From this experience came *Ballads of the Boer
War*, published in 1902. With the war over he was reappointed
Aide-de-Camp and returned to Canada in the spring of 1903.

An Aide-de-Camp is responsible for planning and supervis-
ing the many details in the public life of a viceregal representative. The smoothness and success of a Governor General's
official duties in no small measure reflect the ADC's foresight in
avoiding difficulties before they arise and his adeptness in cop-
ing with the unforeseeable.

Lord Minto's term of office in Canada was a busy one for
himself and, therefore, for his staff. The long and arduous
journey to the Klondike took place in 1900, and in the autumn
of 1901 Their Royal Highnesses the Duke and Duchess of
Cornwall and York, the future King George V and Queen
Mary, made a Royal Tour of Canada. As Queen Victoria had
died in January of that year, the country was still in mourning,
and rules of dress and regulations as to public functions were
strictly followed during the Tour. Captain Graham was the ADC
on the day of Their Royal Highness's arrival and travelled on
the tour with Lady Minto. There were two trains, the Royal
and the viceregal. On the latter Lady Minto and her party were
accompanied by Prime Minister Sir Wilfrid Laurier. Lord

Minto remained in Ottawa but joined His Royal Highness at Poplar Point, Manitoba, for shooting which had been arranged by Senator Kirchhoffer of Brandon.

Besides these long tours and the shorter journeys he so frequently made, the Governor General had a full schedule of formal and official duties at Ottawa.

There was a lighter side to life at Rideau Hall. Lady Minto gave glimpses of this in *Myself When Young*,[1] picturing a large, happy, laughing family, made up of parents, children and staff. Their summers included camping and fishing, their winters skating, skiing and sleighing, as well as parties and theatricals. Soon after the new viceregal household was established in Government House, Ottawa, Harry Graham's special abilities as a musician and dramatist came to the fore. He had inherited these talents from his father, for Sir Henry sang and played songs of his own composition, and had an enormous repertoire of comic songs. Captain Graham not only sang but also wrote and produced plays at Rideau Hall, to be acted by the staff and children. His enthusiasm for theatricals and musicals inspired the amateur actors and brought forth their latent talents.

His first production was *The Babes in the Woods*, and according to Lady Minto it "took Ottawa by storm." In his Diary Lord Minto made note of various productions, describing them as "excellent" or "a tremendous success." In 1904 the last one, *Bluebeard*, ran for three evenings, and the Governor General's Diary described it as "Harry's greatest triumph," stating that among those present were the Siftons and Sir Wilfrid and Lady Laurier, and from Montreal the Cloustons, the Montagues, the Allens and Colin Campbell.

It is not surprising that in writing to Lord Minto on November 18, 1901 (after Captain Graham's departure for active service in South Africa) Sir Henry Graham should express the feeling that his son's "merits and capabilities" had had a "much more genial field for their exercise and development in Canada than at Wellington Barracks."

[1] Margot Asquith, Countess of Oxford and Asquith, ed., *Myself When Young—By Famous Women of Today* (London: Frederick Muller Ltd., 1938).

At times the high spirits of Graham and the rest of the young staff were an embarrassment to the Governor General. In June 1899, urgent business shortened an official visit to Niagara, and though His Excellency was sorry to disappoint the people by missing a ball, he told Lady Minto: "Laurence[2] and Harry behaved disgracefully and it was high time I took them away." Perhaps the greatest aggravation was a poem of Graham's which began:

Theodore Roosevelt
Alert as bird or early worm,
   Yet gifted with those courtly ways
Which connoisseurs correctly term
   The tout-c'qu'-il-y-a de Louis seize;
He reigned, by popular assent,
   The People's peerless President!

Behold him! Squarely built and small;
   With hands that would resemble Liszt's,
Did they not forcibly recall
   The contour of Fitzsimmons' fists.
Beneath his velvet gloves you feel
   The politician's grip of steel.

Accomplished as a King should be,
   And autocratic as a Czar,
To him all classes bowed the knee,
   In spotless Washington afar;
Though jealous rivals dared to scoff,
   He wore the smile-that-won't-come-off.[3]

and continued for twenty-one verses. Lady Minto and Graham (perhaps fortunately) were in England when Lord Minto found out about it. He wrote to his wife:

I am furious at this moment. I hear Harry has written a poem to an American Magazine signed Harry Graham, in which he makes fun of

[2] Laurence Drummond, the Governor General's Military Secretary.

[3] *Misrepresentative Men* (London: Gay and Bird, 1904).

Roosevelt—it really is too bad—no one on my staff ought to write to the press—it ought to be a strictly understood rule—but I thought all the danger was over, and that it might appear like finding fault to forbid it when there was little more chance of it happening—but to sign his name to such a thing I can't conceive. I haven't seen it— Cloche told me of it—Seward Webber having remarked on it as likely to be annoying just before a Presidential Election—It may be perfectly harmless, but it's all wrong for one of my staff to be making fun of the President—I am really annoyed.

On another occasion His Excellency lamented: "Fancy that idiot Harry Graham has lost all the things I gave him to take to England—my skating boots, skates and things for Mathews—it is maddening. I hope from his letter he has made some mistake ... but I always say, the brain of an ADC is an awful thing." It is clear from Lord Minto's private correspondence and his diaries, however, that he delighted in Harry Graham and enjoyed his companionship. In another letter to Lady Minto he wrote: "Harry quite awful and makes me hysterical he is so amusing."

When Lady Minto went to Japan in the fall of 1903 Captain Graham spent a lot of time with His Excellency, both in Ottawa and canoeing, camping and hunting. When Graham left Canada for a holiday in England before her return, Lord Minto wrote to his wife that Harry had been charming and he would miss him very much:

Had a farewell dinner for Harry—his Hill Crest party ... I miss Harry very much—he loves all the girls and they all adore him—I don't think he really much cares for camp life—and I'm sure had quite enough of Kippawa [sic]—but in Ottawa he is excellent and a most amusing companion. I love Comptroller also but he doesn't seem to amalgamate with Ottawa like Harry.

Captain Graham's correspondence must have been a bright spot in official life, too. Perhaps a Canadian influence can be detected in a letter he wrote from London to Lord Minto on June 13, 1901: "I have been home a whole week and find the English climate to be even more poisonous that what I had read about it in books. It has been trying to snow most of the time and the English people seem to prefer to live in thorough draughts and don't understand the very rudiments of house warming." He mentions seeing Lady Minto's friends and giving them glowing accounts of all things Canadian. His letter concludes: "In view of the Coronation the price of ermine is rising rapidly, while white rabbits and black tailed cats are at a premium."

It was while he was an ADC in Canada (1899) that Graham published *Ruthless Rhymes for Heartless Homes*, which delight with their absurdity and irreverence. For example:

The Englishman's Home[4]
I was playing golf the day
   That the Germans landed;
All our troops had run away,
   All our ships were stranded;
And the thought of England's shame
   Altogether spoilt my game.

In June of 1904, the year he published *Misrepresentative Men*, Graham accompanied Lady Minto and her daughter Lady Eileen to England. It was his intention to return to Canada and stay with the Governor General until the end of his term in November, but in London he was offered the position of Private Secretary to Lord Rosebery, former British Prime Minister and man of letters. On July 7, 1904 Graham wrote to Lord Minto from London:

This is only a hurried letter to catch tomorrow's mail, & to tell you the result of my journey to England. I dined with Ld. Rosebery last night & lunched with him today, & spent the afternoon talking to him. He was perfectly charming—& has offered me the Secretaryship, which I have accepted. I told him frankly that I did not want to do household accounts & such things—& he is going to keep another sec. who

[4] *Ruthless Rhymes for Heartless Homes* (London: Edward Arnold, 1899) and *Most Ruthless Rhymes* (London: Edward Arnold, 1974). Reproduced here with the kind permission of the publisher.

will look after this side of the work ... I am sure I am right to take the job and I only hope I shall fill it satisfactorily. I must tell you again how deeply grateful I am to you for having let me come away at this time & I know that owing to the Dundonald trouble it has put you to some inconvenience not having an ADC. It gives me an awful ridge feeling that I shall not be with you to finish up—& shall not be able to say goodbye to my many Canadian friends. I can never forget your extraordinary kindness to me all these years during which I have had the happiness of serving you.

Graham remained with Lord Rosebery for two years, and it was during this time that he met actress Ethel Barrymore. In her autobiography[5] Miss Barrymore describes Harry Graham as "a gay, brilliant creature of great charm and attraction" who used to have tea with her and her brother Jack at their apartment in Charles Street. They had many friends in common and kept meeting in London and on weekends in the country. James Barrie was their host when he had a cricket week of artists versus writers. Miss Barrymore and Graham became engaged and bought a house in London. Miss Barrymore then returned to America. Graham was to follow and they were to be married, but, according to a letter written by a Canadian in London, E.S. Clouston, to Lady Minto, on May 4, 1906, Miss Barrymore had been operated on for appendicitis and had cabled Graham not to come. Graham's mood was unhappy. Clouston continued: "I will believe in the marriage when it comes off as Miss Ethel is rather an uncertain quantity. I would be very sad for him but not an unmixed evil—entre nous." The relationship was of such general speculation as to justify the Ottawa and New York papers carrying news both of the engagement in 1905 and its ending in 1906.

After his retirement from the Army in 1904 and his two years with Lord Rosebery (1904–1906), Harry Graham made writing his career. In the early years he created the unforgettable characters of Mr. Biffin and Lord Bellinger and in 1936, the year he died, he published one of his most hilarious stories,

[5] Ethel Barrymore, *Memories: An Autobiography* (New York: Harper & Brothers, 1955).

The Private Life of Gregory Gorm. His play *Little Miss Nobody* (with music by Arthur E. Godfrey, London Ronald and Paul A. Rubens) was produced at the Lyric Theatre as early as 1901, and by 1914 he was very much a part of the West End theatre life of London. In that year his *State Secrets* was playing at the Criterion Theatre and *The Cinema Star* at the Shaftesbury. Until 1932 he was annually involved with new plays, sometimes as many as four in a year. *The Times* of London of December 10, 1923, lists the then current productions of Graham plays: two companies playing *Whirled into Happiness*, two companies playing *Lady of the Rose* and one each performing *Toni, Sybil* and *Betty in Mayfair* sent on tour from Daly's. *The White Horse Inn*, which Graham freely adapted from a German play and for which he wrote the lyrics, opened at the London Coliseum on April 8, 1931. *The Times* reported that it "took London by storm" and after 651 performances in London went on a long tour. It was revived at the Coliseum in 1940, again went on tour and has since been seen as an ice spectacle.

In 1910 Harry Graham married Dorothy, daughter of Sir Francis Villiers, GCVO, KCMG, Ambassador to Belgium. They had one daughter, Virginia, now Mrs. Antony Thesiger of London, England, who inherited the family talent. She was for years a regular contributor to *Punch* and continues to write for English periodicals. Captain Graham, who disliked ostentation and self-publicity, enjoyed relating that the only picture of him that had ever appeared in the "weekly snob-stuff" press was one with his gifted daughter, the caption for which ran: "Miss Graham and friend."

Harry Graham's serious interest in the arts was reflected in his appointment as a Trustee of the British Museum. He also never lost his interest in and affection for his old regiment, which he rejoined in 1914, seeing active service in France when he was over 40 years of age. To the end, he retained the bearing and characteristics of a military man. "Captain Graham," remarked a stage manager at Daly's one day, "Captain Graham, what I likes about yer is that yer my idea of a fine old English gentleman!"

Harry Graham loved London. He loved working into the small hours of the morning, lunching at his clubs—the Beef-

steak and the Garrick—and sharing the excitement of opening
nights with his wife and daughter. His quiet humour was a
delight to his friends, and his writing added gaiety to the lives
of many. When he died at his London home on October 30,
1936, at the age of 61, there was a long tribute in *The Times* the
following day. In it Lieutenant-Colonel C.P. Hawkes wrote:

It is given to few writers to produce work which so truly and spontane-
ously reflects their personalities that thousands of readers who have
neither seen nor met them seem to know them like personal friends.
Harry Graham enjoyed (in every sense) this rare peculiarity.

Background to the Journey

The Earl of Minto's term as the Queen's representative in Canada was characterized by a serious concern for affairs of state during a significant time in Canada's history.

The new Governor General arrived at Quebec City on November 12, 1898, a few months after the convening of a Joint High Commission which had been created to settle many matters at issue between the United States and Canada. Of these, the Alaska Boundary dispute was of prime importance.

The year 1898 was also the peak year of the gold rush to the Klondike region of the Yukon. George Carmack had discovered gold on Bonanza Creek in August 1896, and although word spread rapidly through the Yukon, it was the next year before the outside world heard about it. By 1898 the full fever of the gold rush had sent thousands flocking to the Yukon.

The stampeders travelled many routes to reach the Klondike. Some chose an overland route from Edmonton, while others went through British Columbia to the headwaters of the Yukon River. Many went by the all-water route via the Pacific Ocean, the Bering Sea and the Yukon River, but passage was difficult to secure, and the Bering Sea in the far North was only open to navigation from late June to September. The majority took the shorter route by water to Dyea and Skagway and thence over the Chilkoot and White Passes. These mountain passes swarmed with people of every sort and condition, hauling mounds of supplies, furniture, stoves, even a piano. Those who survived the gruelling ordeal of the mountains stretched for miles along Lake Lindeman and Lake Bennett, building thousands of boats to transport them the more than five hun-

dred miles down the Yukon River to Dawson City. It was estimated that in May 1898, there were 10,000 men at Lake Bennett, 10,000 at Lake Lindeman and 20,000 others shuttling
their supplies over the trails from Dyea and Skagway.

Such an influx into unorganized territory was bound to give
rise to difficulties of administration, and Lord Minto at once
became interested and involved in the many problems of the
Yukon, particularly the question of the Alaskan border and the
maladministration of the Territory.

The boundary dispute had its origins in 1825 when Russia
and Great Britain signed a Treaty by which Russia received a
long strip of the northwest coast of America, now known as the
Alaskan panhandle. In 1867, the United States bought Alaska,
including the Panhandle, but the exact location of the boundary as designated by the Treaty of 1825 was unclear. The
United States claimed an unbroken line while Canada claimed
gateways in the boundary to give her access to the ocean.

The Joint High Commission into Canadian–American issues
adjourned in February 1899 because of its inability to come to a
decision on the matter of the border. It was scheduled to reconvene in August 1899, but did not, purportedly because
Lord Herschell, the Chairman, and Mr. Dingle, an American
commissioner, both died in the spring of 1899. But the real
reason for its failure to reassemble, as reported by the Governor General to Colonial Secretary Joseph Chamberlain, was
that Sir Wilfrid Laurier would not agree to another meeting of
the Commission until the Alaskan Boundary question was settled. Great Britain had agreed to arbitration in the matter of
Venezuela and the Nicaraguan (Panama) Canal, where American and British interests were in conflict, and Canada felt that
the same type of arbitration should be used to delineate the
Alaskan Boundary.

Lord Minto's Scrapbook of newspaper clippings, as well as
his correspondence, shows how carefully he followed the situation. He was aware of the uncompromising attitude of the
United States, of Great Britain's desire and need for United
States friendship, and of the animosity felt by Canadians toward the United States. In a letter to Queen Victoria, dated
May 11, 1899, he told her that the friendly feeling in England

for the United States was not reciprocated in Canada and that he thought that since Canada was a near neighbour its views might be more correct than those formed across the Atlantic. He expressed his anxiety "lest the rapprochement [of Great Britain] with the United States may be taken here to mean a want of appreciation of Canadian Sympathies."

The Joint High Commission having failed to reconvene, a provisional agreement was arrived at in October 1899, which gave the United States command of the sea ports and Canada command of the mountain passes. This was the *modus vivendi* in 1900 when Lord Minto and his viceregal party set off for the Yukon.

The maladministration of the Yukon Territories had been the subject of general conversation ever since the new Governor General's arrival in Canada. Miners and newspaper reporters returning from the gold fields brought stories of abuses there, and the Conservative opposition in Ottawa was quick to pick them up and make the complaints the central issue in the parliamentary session of 1899. Lord Minto wrote to the Queen:

Parliament opened with a very long debate on the address, the speeches being cruelly long. Sir Charles Tupper, leader of the Opposition speaking for 6–3/4 hours and his son following him with 7 hours, the chief discussion turning on the maladministration of affairs in the Yukon district. The Government however have weakened the attack, though I am much inclined to think the mangement [sic] of affairs in the Gold Districts would not bear very close scrutiny.

The Yukon Territory in theory was governed by a Commissioner and Council, but in fact the Minister of the Interior, Clifford Sifton, controlled it almost singlehandedly, making all appointments from Ottawa. It was his officials who allotted claims and collected royalties, controlled the liquor trade and governed the Territory. The criticism of the Yukon administration, therefore, was pretty much a criticism of Sifton, and stories were circulated that he and his friends were making fortunes.

The Opposition demanded an official investigation. Sifton

refused to authorize one on the basis of rumours based on anonymous sources, but said he would agree if specific charges were laid by persons identifying themselves. No one came forward, so Sifton had William Ogilvie, his own appointee as the Commissioner of the Territory, investigate the matter. The results were negative.

Meanwhile the Governor General was receiving direct requests from the Yukon for reform, including resolutions sent to him by Joseph Clarke, secretary for a mass meeting of Yukon citizens held on May 5, 1900.

On the eve of a general election, therefore, Sir Wilfrid Laurier found himself in a situation where the wealth of the gold mines was overshadowed by the unsolved boundary dispute and an accusation of mismanagement of the Yukon involving a Minister of the Crown who was very important to the Prime Minister's plans for the future development of the country. So on July 19, 1900, Lord and Lady Minto left Ottawa to travel thousands of miles across the Dominion and north to Dawson City, where he gathered first-hand information with which to inform his ministers and, in Laurier's words, "inspired the people of that distant land with the hope that their legitimate grievances would at length be remedied."

ACROSS CANADA TO THE KLONDYKE

Dedicated to *Their Excellencies*

The journey ends;
   We turn and gaze
  Down the long vista of the days,
  Since first we joined our common ways
   And shared our common weather.
The path extends,
   From shore to shore,
  Ten times ten hundred miles—and more,
  The days stretch out, a full four score,
   Those days we spent together.

But, tho' the journey end at last,
Tho' Time may blur the scene, and cast
Its jealous shadows o'er the past,
   One thought shall make amends;
One touch of happiness shall be
Treasured and blest and dear to me,
The ever golden memory
   That we were friends!

H.G.
1900

Contents

PART I

TO THE WEST

Chapter 1

July 19th to 28th

Ottawa to Banff. The start from Ottawa. North Bay. Fort William. Rat Portage. Lake of the Woods. The Sultana Gold Mine. Arrival at Winnipeg. Opening of the Exhibition. A Scotch Concert. The Manitoba Club Dinner. Reception in the Parliament Buildings. The Prairie. Regina. Moose Jaw. The Bow River. Calgary. The Rockies. Banff. The Sulphur and Hot Springs. The National Park. "Devil's Lake."

July 19th, 1900

This is the date finally settled upon for our departure from Ottawa, and, at about one P.M. to-day, in the various vehicles ordered for the purpose, we drive down to the railway station.

Passing through the still bare and blackened scene of the great Ottawa Fire, we arrive at the Canadian Pacific Railway Union Depot, which has risen phoenix-like from its ashes, and where we receive the farewells and good wishes of the many friends who have come to see us off.

The sun shines brightly down as we take our seats, and, in a few minutes, the journey is begun, and we are steaming slowly westwards in the train which is to be our home and headquarters for so long a period.

The party consists of Their Excellencies, The Governor General of Canada and Lady Minto, and their personal staff, comprising the Comptroller of the Household, the Private Secretary, the Aide-de-Camp, and seven servants. And here perhaps

Left to right: The Private Secretary, Arthur Sladen; The Comptroller, Arthur Guise; The Earl of Minto; The Aide-de-Camp, Captain Harry Graham (Col. D. Streamer); Lady Minto.

it would be just as well to give a short description of the Vice-Regal Staff, difficult as it must inevitably be to enumerate, in a few short and concise sentences, their several leading characteristics, as they appear to the humble chronicler of these pages.

The Comptroller[1] is a wild, warmhearted Irishman. Good looking, good natured; long headed, long legged, and short tempered; intolerant and kindly. A character which combines sound common sense with a passion for illogical argument. A firm friend, and he has many friends; a generous foe, and he has no enemies. Broadminded on most points, and these the large issues of life; violently prejudiced on others, and these the petty controversies unworthy the labour of discussion. Quick to anger, and as quick to the deepest remorse. Headstrong, impetuous, and an invariable partisan to the unpopular view of any question. To a singular faculty for misplacing names he adds a studied forgetfulness of faces, a talent which he carries almost to the level of a fine art. In private an earnest and interesting talker, he yet possesses, for the purposes of

[1] W. Arthur Guise (son of General Guise v.c.) came to Canada with Lord Minto in 1898. A letter of recommendation from the Earl of Crewe, whose private secretary Guise had been, describes Guise as "a charming fellow personally ... [who] gets on with everybody." (The numbered footnotes throughout the text were added by the editor. Those with asterisks are Captain Graham's.)

general conversation, an inexhaustible stream of the "fluent obvious" which is absolutely invaluable for tiding over the agonizing pauses which are apt to punctuate the family meals of the best-regulated household. His features are immoveable and can at times assume an expression reminiscent of the vegetable existence of a prehistoric glacial period, but his long artistic hands have almost solved the theory of perpetual motion. A bonviveur of bohemian tastes, an Imperialist with radical tendencies, an absolutely unselfish man ingrained with the cynicism of a lifelong dissatisfaction with his lot. Ever ready with sympathy for others; seeking sympathy from none. Possessing an unusual faculty for enjoyment, the highest powers of pleasure and the sternest sense of duty.

The Private Secretary[2] is an elderly young man of thirty-five; married and settled down to a life which he takes most seriously. Modest and unassuming; but strong-willed, with the consciousness of hidden power. Curious and receptive of information, and anxious to impart of it to others; to him the world is an open garden of knowledge where he may gather facts. Conscientious and possessed of a sound common sense, which enables him to sift diverging opinions, and obtain a golden mean of decision. Work is his favourite occupation, after which he prefers to do nothing. He boasts of no religious opinions, but has strong views on morality, and combines a taste for lemonade with leanings toward total abstinence, leanings manfully resisted and successfully overcome. Possessed of a strong sporting instinct, games of chance have a fatal fascination for him, and he has been heard to state that champagne is the only wine he ever drinks. He has no small talk at his command, but is an excellent and ready listener, the result no doubt of early training in Her Majesty's Royal Marines.

The Aide-de-Camp[3] is a Scotchman by birth, an Englishman by occupation. Quick of imagination, slow of decision. Good

---

[2] Arthur F. Sladen, son of Col. Joseph Sladen, born and educated in England, emigrated to Canada. In 1890 he entered the Governor General's office in Ottawa as a clerk, became Lord Minto's private secretary and served in the same capacity until 1926, with four succeeding Governors General.

[3] The author of the Journal, "Col. D. Streamer" (Captain Harry Graham).

tempered, reserved, and constitutionally disinclined to exertion. Sensible, sensitive, and selfish. With the ambition to succeed, but without the energy necessary to success. Not sufficiently interested in life to be an enthusiast; not disinterested enough to be a humanitarian. Impatient of stupidity in others, unconscious of it in himself. With the highest possible animal spirits dominated at times by a profound melancholy. A dilettante with a turn for writing inferior doggerel, a taste for literature, an ear for music, a retentive memory and a prodigious thirst.

Besides the Governor General's official car "Victoria," a sleeping car and a baggage car have been provided for the use of the travellers.

The private car "Victoria" consists of a diningroom and drawingroom, one at either end, three fair sized bedrooms, and a small kitchen where our faithful coloured cook, Daniel, produces, on all occasions, the most toothsome meals at the shortest notice. The car itself is under the special supervision of Staff-Sergeant Rogers, now for some twenty-five years Orderly to succeeding Governors General; a man of many parts, whose genial smile is known and welcomed all over the Dominion.

The first day is spent in settling down for the long journey. The Aide-de-Camp, in a fit of absence of mind, has his luggage put into the best cabin on the private car, after which he is very free with his advice to the Comptroller and Private Secretary as to what portion of the floor in the sleeping car they would find most convenient and comfortable for the arrangement of their humble resting places. In the end all is amicably settled and mutual recriminations temporarily cease.

The scenery at first is picturesque, but grows, after a time, monotonous. Mile after mile of well-watered, well-wooded country, somewhat reminiscent of the South of Ireland, with no sign of animal life to break the dead level of similarity, soon wearies the eye.

Towards five P.M. the Private Secretary states that he saw a bird. He refuses to divulge anything further upon the subject, but, on being pressed, declares that, as a matter of fact, he also noticed, about an hour ago, what appeared to him to be the

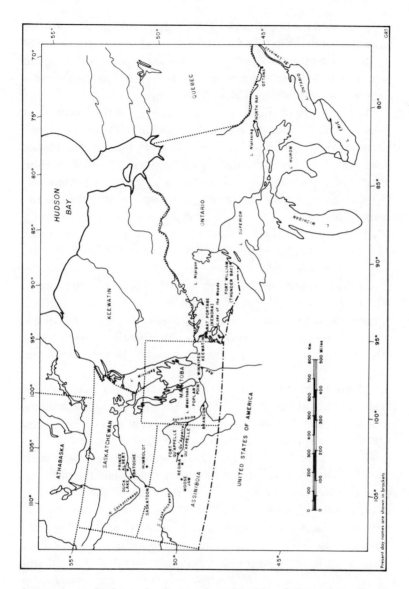

foot-prints of a bear, in the sand at the side of the railway line.
(The following cross-examination ensues, the Private Secretary
being warned that anything he may say will be taken down,
altered and used in evidence against him. *Question:* What did
you do? *Answer:* Nothing. *Question:* Had you been drinking?
Answer: No. *Question:* Why not? *Answer:* Because at that time I

had not seen the bear tracks.) The Comptroller talking upon the question of drink, a very favorite one with him, says that he fully expects to be partially under the influence of alcohol during the entire trip, because, when travelling, so he affirms, plain water is never safe. His advice evidently is to "let well alone."

At about eight thirty P.M. we stop for twenty minutes at North Bay, on the shore of Lake Nipissing. There is a crowd here waiting to see the Governor General, but His Excellency and the Aide-de-Camp disembark unostentatiously from the rear end of the car and walk about the platform unrecognised. One of the would-be sightseers, after looking into the car for some time without success, is heard to remark disappointedly that he supposes His Excellency is "travelling under the seat." This theory is apparently accepted as the correct one, and the crowd gradually fades away.

As night draws on the scenery grows wilder and more hilly: the line curves with greater frequency, and its course grows gradually more elliptical. On being asked what he thinks of the country the Private Secretary states that he "hasn't quite thought"; it looks full of game, he says, but he hasn't seen any yet.

The only thing of interest that the Comptroller has noticed is the corridor of flowers through which we have been travelling all day. Cross examined as to what kind of flowers, he answers, "Pink," and refuses to commit himself further.

The Private Secretary has also observed a large number of lilypads growing along the line, and states that they are the favorite food of the moose, who eat them by the roots. The Comptroller denies this, and says that moose subsist entirely upon the bark of trees. Hence the Canadian sport of "moose-calling," in which the Indians are so skilled. The Indian, according to the Comptroller, conceals himself in a wood and gives vent to a weird cry, towards which the thoughtless moose, mistaking it for the bark upon which he loves to browse, hurries along with an expectant smile. When the moose arrives within a few feet of the Indian, this nobleman proceeds to blow him up with a shotgun, and the evening's sport is at an end.

All day long, says the Private Secretary, he hasn't seen a

single partridge. (Cross-examined. *Question:* Have you been drinking? *Answer:* No.) He thinks, however, that on the surface of the lake, he saw a loon; as he says this he looks meaningly at the Aide-de-Camp, who is taking off his boots preparatory to retiring for the night. The look, however, is intercepted by the Comptroller, who laughs through his nose in an offensive manner, and receives one of the aforementioned boots at his head for his trouble.

July 20th

A cool pleasant day. In the early morning the Comptroller is heard accusing the Private Secretary in bitter terms of misappropriating a portion of his hairwash for his own private use. This the Private Secretary denies emphatically, and further asserts that he never uses anything for his head at all, having got to the age when, like the late Count Bismarck, he can part his hair with a towel.

At Fort William, where our longest stop is made, we get out and walk about. An external inspection of the car "Victoria" shows that it needs revarnishing badly. The Comptroller is against this, saying that it isn't worth it. When questioned, he asserts that, as a matter of fact, the car "isn't safe anyhow" and that varnish would be wasted on such an unworthy object. The prospect of travelling for some weeks upon a car that "isn't safe anyhow" is not cheering, but we are encouraged to proceed upon our journey by the knowledge that, like others of his countrymen, the Comptroller is apt at times to rely upon his imagination for his facts.

We learn to-day that our cook is very unwell. The Private Secretary says he thinks that, from the symptoms, he must be suffering from gastric juice. He admits ignorance upon medical matters, but fancies that this disease is the result of chewing unripe tobacco. He recommends that a hot bottle be applied to the affected part, and suggests the name of the Aide-de-Camp as a suitable applicant. The latter, however, fails to see the point of this, and bed time brings to a close an argument which threatens to grow too heated to be salutary.

We awake to find ourselves at Rat Portage, where we are to spend the day. (The Private Secretary, in a frivolous moment, calls it "Mouse Run," but is silenced by a stern glance from the Aide-de-Camp, and, for the moment, retires within himself and draws down the blinds.)

Rat Portage is a small town of about five thousand inhabitants, situated on the famous Lake of the Woods, a vast piece of water containing some ten thousand islands and much patronized by holiday-makers and tourists.

The Comptroller is up early, and sees several Indians, the first we have hitherto met. He notices one small one with a large gun, whose bloodthirsty appearance rather frightens him, but he pretends to be indifferent to the presence of the noble Red Man, and so, no doubt, escapes with his scalp. The Private Secretary meanwhile has seen a squaw wearing her papoose on a board strapped to her back, and is proportionately thrilled. The Aide-de-Camp sees nothing, having remained in bed until nine A.M. so as to give the others a chance.

At nine-thirty A.M. the Mayor and several prominent citizens board the car. They express the kind intention of taking us for a trip on the lake, and at ten-thirty we start off on board Lieutenant-General Sir Henry Wilkinson's[4] palatial houseboat, towed by the *Clipper*.

Our course is nearly due south, through "The Devil's Gap," a small passage, not more than forty yards wide, through which the water from a chain of lakes, two hundred miles long, passes, and where some humourist has painted a portrait of His Satanic Majesty upon the face of an adjacent rock. Our first stopping place is the Sultana Gold Mine, over which we are shown by the courteous Manager, Mr. Strong. This mine is worked almost entirely by Swedes, whose wages average about two dollars and a half per day, and who, in blue working suit, and broad-brimmed hat, in which is fixed a naked candle, appear as contented as they are picturesque.

[4] Lieutenant-General Sir Henry Wilkinson was the Chairman and Managing Director of the Regina (Canada) Gold Mine Company of London, England.

Sir Henry Wilkinson provides an excellent mid-day repast upon his houseboat, to which the Comptroller invites himself; but the Private Secretary and Aide-de-Camp, with humbler tastes, prefer to seek their food in the hospitable cabin of the *Clipper*. Here a luncheon of beef and blueberry pie is satisfactorily consumed, and the Private Secretary indiscreetly partakes of a cucumber salad, at the bottom of which a perfect nest of onions lies concealed. It is this fact more than any other that causes him to shun the society of his fellowmen during the afternoon, and he sits apart, with a brooding and regretful air, which evokes universal compassion and sympathy.

After luncheon we proceed to Keewatin, where stands the largest flour manufactory in Canada, operated by the "Lake of the Woods Milling Company." Mr. Kelly, the Manager, shows us round this interesting factory, where machinery capable of turning out three thousand barrels of flour per day is working at full pressure, and we learn that it only requires the services of five men to keep this wonderful aggregation of mechanism perpetually in working order and at work.

The road to and from the mill is made exclusively of saw-dust, which does not seem an altogether happy choice of mate-rial, covering and filling, as it does, the clothes and lungs with fine particles of wood, which are neither ornamental nor healthful, and which are equally irritating to eyesight and temper.

In the course of conversation with an intellectual native the Aide-de-Camp discovers the source from which the town of Rat Portage derives its name. It appears, according to the sworn affidavit of this apparently incorruptible man, that there is a small strip of land leading from the Lake of the Woods to the Winnipeg River, and that, at certain seasons of the year, when the former was frozen over, all the four-footed animals, mink, otters, and rats, would collect their goods and chattels together and "portage" them across this space from lake to river. Such was the number of these itinerants that they even-tually wore a groove with their tails in the bare rock, and so suggested a suitable name to the founder of the little village, which now so deeply regrets its nomenclature.[5]

The scenery in the Lake very much resembles that of the Thousand Islands in the St. Lawrence, but, for general charm and beauty of situation, the latter, in many opinions, bears away the palm.

We leave Rat Portage at four-thirty P.M. amid the cheers of the assembled populace. "God Save the Queen" is sung as we steam out of the station, the National Anthem being led by an old English veteran who thus finds an opportunity of express-ing his patriotism and loyalty in no uncertain tones.

[5] The town was incorporated under the name of "Kenora" in 1904, the name being obtained by taking the first two letters of three separate Lake of the Woods settlements, Keewatin, Norman and Rat Portage.

We arrive here tonight at eight-thirty P.M. and are met at the station by the Officers of The District, the Mayor and leading officials.

After a short stay in the waiting room, His Honour the Lieutenant Governor of Manitoba, the Premier of the Province, and several Ministers appear upon the scene.

A carriage with four grey horses stands in readiness, in which Their Excellencies, His Honour, and the Aide-de-Camp take their seats and are driven to the City Hall.

A torchlight procession accompanies the party, and the music of a score of bands makes night harmonious. All along the route the houses are brilliantly illuminated, and the gardens are gay with bunting and decorations. Thousands of people line the streets and welcome the Governor General with a warmth of enthusiasm unparalleled within the memory of the oldest inhabitant.[6]

At the Civic Hall the Mayor presents an address, and the procession once more heads off for Government House. Excited by the wild plaudits of the populace, and by the glare of torches and occasional pyrotechnic display of the youth of the town, the leaders in the Vice-Regal equipage become unmanageable and have to be unharnessed and sent home. After a short delay the carriage proceeds, with two horses, and eventually reaches Government House, after a drive of two miles which has taken about two hours in the accomplishing. The orderliness of the great crowd is truly remarkable, and we learn with interest that, in this town of fifty thousand inhabitants, only eighteen policemen are required to keep the peace. "English Provincial press please copy."

[6] "I hope the English papers have said something of our reception at Winnipeg. It really was wonderful. The Canadians are not a demonstrative people—they are always accused of not being able to cheer, and are very apt to pretend not to see you rather than take their hats off—but at Winnipeg they fairly broke through all restrictions." (Letter of Lord Minto to Arthur Elliot, July 31, 1900. Public Archives of Canada.)

Left to right: Lt. Col. C.M. Boswell, Commanding Officer, 90th Winnipeg Rifles 1887–1895; Lord Minto; Captain Graham.

Sunday, July 22nd. Winnipeg

Today we take a well-earned rest until luncheon time. In the afternoon we go to Church at Holy Trinity,[7] where a parade service is being held for the troops of the garrison. The Private Secretary is unable to attend, owing to a pressing business engagement which keeps him chained to his bed till well

[7] "On Sunday afternoon, Trinity Church was filled to overflowing with, I am afraid, not worshippers. Lady Minto being the cynosure of all curiosity, overcame religion, and her looks, clothes and manners were discussed very audibly during the service, and it was decided she looked every inch a Countess. She wore a beautiful street gown of white, with turquoise blue touches, and carried a blue parasol." (*Town Topics*, Winnipeg, July 28, 1900. Provincial Archives of Manitoba.)

on in the forenoon, and which necessitates his remaining at home for the rest of the day to write letters of great importance, in time, so he says, to catch the mail, which, as he omits to remark, doesn't leave on Sunday at all.

His Excellency and the Aide-de-Camp march to and from Church with the troops, at the head of the 90th Battalion, of which His Excellency is the Honorary Lieutenant-Colonel, and, the day being hot, they arrive perspiring, and sufficiently irritable to be annoyed at the discovery of an imminent collection. The Comptroller is fortunately provided with the necessary funds, which he lends to all, in sufficient quantities, to put, as he flippantly terms it, "in the pool."

An excellent discourse is delivered by the Archbishop of Rupert's Land, a region which, in the Comptroller's opinion, consists entirely of ice. As usual the Aide-de-Camp informs him of the extent of his crass ignorance in time to avoid a public shame, and so saves the honour and reputation of the Vice-Regal household.

A large dinner at Government House closes the day satisfactorily.

July 23rd

Breakfast is fortunately a moveable feast here, some of us preferring to feed at an early hour, while others stroll into the diningroom at ten A.M.

The Comptroller solves the difficulty by not coming down at all until the sun is high in the heavens.

At one-thirty His Excellency, the Private Secretary, and Aide-de-Camp, attended by an escort of the Royal Canadian Dragoons, drive to the Exhibition Grounds, where a large and long luncheon is consumed, and where His Excellency finally declares the Winnipeg Fair of 1900 formally opened. In the afternoon Her Excellency and the Comptroller arrive for tea, and His Excellency joins them at the refreshment room, in time to be offered a beverage in which coffee and tea are genially but mistakenly mixed, but which he nevertheless gallantly consumes.

This evening His Excellency, the Private Secretary, and

22 Aide-de-Camp dine with the Manitoba Club. A most enjoyable evening, an excellent dinner and excellent speechmaking, both short and to the point. Her Excellency and the Comptroller are meanwhile taken by the Lieutenant Governor to revisit the fair, where a display of fireworks is one of the features of the evening.

July 24th

Today the Private Secretary and Comptroller decline to do any duty whatever, and spend a happy time among the "freaks" at the Exhibition. They are particularly attracted by the "Ossified Man" and lose their hearts to the "hairy lady from Honolulu." They are almost induced by the "boneless wonder of Buenos Ayres" to attach themselves permanently to the freakshow, but the terms offered them are apparently insufficient, and they somewhat regretfully return to Government House in time for dinner.

Meanwhile Their Excellencies, His Honour and the Aide-de-Camp have visited the hospitals and a Scotch concert given at a theatre, at all of which they have gladdened the hearts of many sufferers by the light of their presence.

One is almost inclined to agree to the accusation of lack of humour, so often brought against the Scotch nation, when he has to listen, for the best part of the afternoon of a lovely summer's day, to long ballads, in the minor key, relating to incidents in the lives of "Angus McDonald," "Argyle Mary" and other estimable personages about whose private family affairs the comparative stranger can have but little personal interest. The singing today is excellent, although one of the performers pleads guilty to an affection of the throat, which the Lieutenant Governor facetiously refers to as a "gathering of the Clans."

His Honour Lieutenant Governor Patterson has only one failing, and that is an appalling generosity, which causes him to give away everything that he possesses. While a guest in his house it is absolutely unsafe to admire his pictures or praise his cigars, as he invariably insists upon at once making you a present of the object of your praise or admiration. If you say that his champagne is excellent, which it certainly is, you find twelve dozen bottles ready packed in your room on the day of your departure. If you chance to commend the tone of his grand piano, he will have it delivered at your house within a week, and the extent of his hospitality and the boundlessness of his generosity become, after a short visit, almost overwhelming.

This evening Their Excellencies give a Reception, open to all comers, in the Parliament Buildings. It is not largely attended, owing to insufficient advertising, shortness of notice and a greater attraction at the Opera House, but it is to be hoped that it gives a certain amount of pleasure to those who can find the time and the disposition to be present.

At eleven P.M. the party leave Government House for the car, where the night is spent, and in which we depart the next morning, deeply sorry to say goodbye to the City which has given us such a welcome, most regretful of leaving the "Liberty Hall" where we have been made so comfortable, and yet more sad to bid adieu to the kindly host whose bounteous hospitality we have so enjoyed.

July 25th

Today we are travelling through mile after mile of prairie and the eye wearies after a time at the dead level of invariable monotony.

The Private Secretary is much disappointed that the bounding prairie doesn't bound in the least; it doesn't even roll, but is unutterably vast and flat. He wouldn't live on it, so he says, not for the world, as he is afraid that in time his nature and his mind might follow suit. His feet are flat already.

The Comptroller misses the trees, and, though he admits to the presence of a number of small undersized shrubs, of uncertain growth and origin, he considers them beneath notice, owing to their not being "big enough to hide behind." This desire for personal concealment seems to indicate a guilty conscience, which is not compatible with the responsibilities of a Comptroller's position.

At Regina (five P.M.) the country grows even more desolate and bare, and there is not even a shrub to refresh the weary plain-tired eye. The reason for the selection of this spot as the site of a town will always remain a mystery, as it would be almost impossible to find a more unloveable "flat and unprofitable" position. The mystery which surrounds the choice, by any sane white man, of this town for his earthly habitation is even more deeply shrouded and incomprehensible. There can be nothing to do here in the way of amusement except, perhaps, play billiards. It would be almost absurd to go out for a ride, as it is never possible to get out of sight of one's own front door. There is no privacy, because your neighbour, even though he be ten miles off, can, from his window, observe you hanging out the clothes in your garden, or hoeing your turnips, and can almost see what you are having for dinner.

One would be inclined to believe that, at the creation of the world, Providence suffered from some sort of temporary mental aphasia when the manufacture of this particular part of the country had to be undertaken, and determined to do nothing at all, but just to leave it flat and unmade. After five or six hundred miles of this inaction a twinge of conscience must have intervened, rousing every effort for the creation of the wonderful country which surrounds the Rocky Mountains.

At Regina the Lieutenant Governor of the North West Territories and Madame Forget board the car, have tea with us and travel in our company as far as the next stopping place, "Moose Jaw," an abridged edition of the Indian name for the place, which signifies "The-Creek-where-the-white-man-mended-the-cart-with-a-moose-jaw-bone," a rather too lengthy appelation for these practical times. Here we learn that the Indians of the Muscow-Petung Reserve are out on the warpath and that an exceptionally large posse of the North West Mounted Police have been sent off to calm them down.

We see the troopers of the North West Mounted Police at most stations, and their smart appearance, in red tunics, dark breeches with yellow stripes, big boots and forage caps or helmets, is most impressive and soldier-like, and must strike terror into the heart of any rebellious Redman.

Soon after this we come upon our first prairie fire, a very

small one, which the Aide-de-Camp hastens to proclaim a
fraud. His idea of such a thing turns out to be a living mass of
flame, extending for a thousand miles in every direction, and
about a hundred yards high. When the settler sees it coming he
mounts his fiery mustang, puts his wife on the pummel in front
of him, his baby in one pocket and his dog in the other, and
gallops for days, pursued by the fiery elements. As the flames
gain upon him he sacrifices his wife, baby and dog, in whatever
order his affection demands, or the state of weariness of his
steed dictates, and at last escapes by plunging into the foaming
rapids of an adjacent torrent.

Our prairie fire is, however, of such a ridiculously inadequate nature that the only inclination of the observer is to walk
up to the thing and blow it out. The Comptroller even goes so
far as to offer to quench the conflagration, if someone will run
and get him a bottle of soda water, but this liquid is too precious for such a purpose, and is forthwith put to the use for
which nature intended it.

July 26th

As we cross the Bow River the whole landscape changes,
prairie giving way to undulating land, well watered and clothed
in trees and shrubs. The prospect is very grateful to the eye
and soothing to the brain.

Occasional ranches are to be seen, with horses and cattle
grazing round, and all the country speaks of prosperity and
plenty.

It begins to rain as we approach Calgary, a little city nestling on a plateau, under the protecting shadow of the Rocky
Mountains. This stupendous range commences at Kananaskis,
with an abruptness that is positively startling, and we soon
find ourselves entering the famous Gap, after which a magnificent view of the Three Sisters and Wind Mountain can be
obtained, and the scenery grows grander and more impressive every moment.

The rain lashes the mountain sides with occasional gusts of
fury, between which assaults the sun peers out, for a moment,

from behind the gathering clouds, and burnishes the rugged, castellated rocks until they shine again.

We arrive at Banff at noon and are met by a four-horsed police-waggon and an escort of the North West Mounted Police under Inspector Wilson. Behind this team which is admirably handled by the constable on the box, and accompanied by this escort, whose gay trappings gleam in the sunshine which is now bursting through the clouds, we are driven to the Banff Springs Hotel, where every effort has been made to secure our comfort.

While standing on the verandah before luncheon an animal, which the Comptroller takes to be a mountain goat, alights upon his hand. On further inspection it turns out to be a particularly large and vulgar looking mosquito and we soon find that the woods swarm with these pests, and that the Hotel itself is by no means free from them.

In the afternoon the whole party drives in a four-in-hand police-cart up Tunnel Mountain, a road which requires iron nerve for the passengers and skill of no mean order for the coachman. Her Excellency subsequently Kodaks the driver, telling him that she wants a picture of "the finest whip in the North West," after which piece of flattery he visibly grows four inches taller, and rumour has it that he concludes the evening, at the bar of the local saloon, in a celebration fitting for such an occasion. We drive home via Sundance Canyon, where the Comptroller picks two wild gooseberries, and is as excited as a

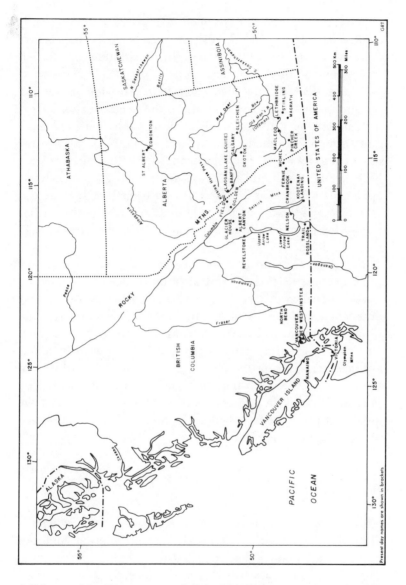

child over his discovery, and visit the famous Sulphur Springs
on our way. Here we are shown the Cave and Basin, in which
the natural warm water bubbles up from the bowels of the
earth, and where the rheumatic patients of the neighbourhood
disport themselves daily, to the enrichment of the proprietor
and the improvement of their own health. We are not induced

to have a bath, the Comptroller saying that it is too much trouble to undress, and the Private Secretary assuring us that there is nothing so detrimental to the constitution as to have a bath when you don't want one.

On the way home the Inspector tells us gruesome stories of a certain species of fly to be found in the neighbourhood. It is nicknamed the Bull-dog, and, in all its habits, puts the mosquito quite in the shade. This animal, so the Inspector assures us, is apt to fly straight at your head, seize a huge piece of your flesh in his mouth and fly away again, leaving a gap in your epidermis which is as undesirable as it is painful. If there are such beasts as this about, the Aide-de-Camp affirms that he has no use for them whatever, and that anyone who cares to may have his share.

Tonight we attend a short concert in the Hotel, given by Mlle. Antoinette Trebelli and M. Eugene Berns. Most of the guests appear at this, some apparently to hear the music, and others to whisper at the back of the room together. There is the usual contingent of elderly matrons, of some sixty summers, who knit everlasting altar-cloths and crochet heartbreaking antimacassars during the performance, and who hardly seem to rest from their self-imposed labours even at meals. The perpetual use of their fingers does not, however, seem to have any effect upon the free working of their tongues and they are as voluble as they are industrious.

July 27th

This morning we hear with great regret that His Excellency is very unwell, having apparently caught an internal chill and being for the moment hors de combat. Talking about chills the Private Secretary says that he heard a sneeze outside his door last night, at a late hour. He at once classified this interruption to his slumbers as a female sneeze, the note being higher and the tone more sustained than is the case with the male explosion. He locked his door at once, but, on thinking better of it, looked out into the passage and observed that the proprietress of the sneeze was somewhat comely in appearance. He immediately set his door ajar and whistled loudly to himself. (Cross-examined. *Question:* What did you whistle? Was it "Come into the garden Maud"? *Answer:* No. I think it was the old ballad "Mother's teeth are plugged with zinc.")

The Private Secretary's repertoire of song is limited to a few religious ditties such as "locked in the stable with the Sheep" or "When Shepherds wash their socks by night," and his method of rendering even these is far from pleasing, so it is not to be wondered at that, on this occasion, his sibylline discords were wholly unsuccessful in their object.

After breakfast the Comptroller, Private Secretary and Aide-de-Camp borrow horses from the North West Mounted Police and go for a ride in the woods. The Mexican saddles supplied are not very comfortable, and it requires some little practice to avoid being rubbed and chafed. The Private Secretary, who hasn't mounted a horse for thirteen years, suffers severely from abrasion of the cuticle, and it will be some days before he resumes anything but a vertical position with pleasure.

We ride up the hill to the Hot Springs, where we are induced to taste the water. The Comptroller assures us that it is the most excellent thing for indigestion, but, after drinking some of it, we unanimously agree that, of the two evils, the indigestion is infinitely the most preferable. These Springs are a sort of modern Lourdes, where the sick of every kind go to be miraculously recovered of their diseases. The little inn contains an autograph book of miracles, in which many happy patients have registered the state of their health on arrival and the swiftness of their respective cures.

In the afternoon Her Excellency and suite are taken in a small launch for a cruise up the Bow River. It rains and is decidedly cold, and the Private Secretary and Aide-de-Camp, who are sitting in the bow, get the full benefit of the malodorous smell of naphtha which pours out in a continuous stream from the engine room. They try to drown dull care in slumber and cigars, but are somewhat glad when, after a cruise of one and a half hours, they reach dry land again, and disembark from what Her Excellency calls the "menthol launch."

After dinner we all go out to see the Bow Falls by moonlight. There is no moon, but, at this season of the year, it remains sufficiently light to be able to read a book at ten P.M., and the falls, which are within a few hundred yards of the Hotel, are well worth a visit. The view from the foot of the rapids looking down from Bow Valley is magnificent, and the rugged summit of the mountain, appropriately termed "Razorback," stands grandly silhouetted against the gradually darkening sky.

Having feasted our eyes sufficiently upon the numerous beauties which Nature here has provided for our satisfaction, we retire to bed, with a happy feeling of elation at being some forty-five hundred feet above the level of the sea, and consequently able to look down somewhat pityingly at less fortunate mortals who must be content with sleeping upon the more humble basement of the world.

July 28th

We are all up early this morning and plunge into the swimming tank of the Hotel, which is warm and sulphurous. Here we disport ourselves for about half an hour "In puris naturalibus," a condition which greatly fusses the caretaker, who declares himself liable to a fine of $25 should we be discovered in this simple costume, and further adds that anyone of us could obtain a reward of $10 for informing against him.

At eleven-thirty A.M., His Excellency being still in bed, the remainder of the party drive out along the bank of the Bow River for a distance of some eight miles. The views are magnificent at every point and the road runs through glades of small firtrees relieved by patches of what appears to be crimson and yellow pernettia, and dotted about with bluebells and michaelmas daisies. Whenever we come to an open space great masses of yellow gallardia brighten the turf, and "painter's brush" can be counted by the thousand, on every side, in flaming rows.

As we drive along the river the Private Secretary says that it reminds him forcibly of Palestine. On being further questioned he admits to never having visited that country, but says that he has read a lot about it in a book. (Cross examined. *Question:* What book? *Answer:* The Bible.) The Comptroller makes a mental determination to borrow one when he gets home and read up the subject.

Silver shrubs, somewhat resembling the English black-thorn, line the water's edge, and, at intervals, we come across high cones of mud and clay, natural formations which the Indians have christened "Hoodoos" and which they no doubt consider as visitors from the spirit world.

The country here must look lovely in the winter, although there is never more than six inches of snow upon the plains in these parts. The Comptroller states that the Chinook wind from the west prevents the snow from deepening, and, when asked why its effect is not felt further east, supposes that, by the time it reaches Winnipeg, it is thoroughly dissipated. The Private Secretary obviously points out that in this particular the Chinook and the Comptroller bear an extraordinary similarity to one another, but is not allowed to carry the comparison any further.

This afternoon, His Excellency having recovered, we are all taken by Mr. Douglas, the Government Agent and Superintendent of the Banff National Park, to see the small herd of wild buffalo which are kept in the vicinity. We manage to drive up quite close to them, as well as to a pair of magnificent elk, which are also living wild in the big park set apart for their use, and Her Excellency, with great bravery, goes up to them and secures several excellent Kodaks. These buffalo are the few survivors of a race which is otherwise extinct in the Dominion, and one is happy to learn that year by year they are increasing in numbers and that there is consequently no fear of the breed eventually dying out.

The drive is then continued along the Hog's Back, and across the Devil's Canyon, a deep rugged gorge through which a torrent of water flows from the Devil's Lake. Here a stop is made for tea at "Beach House" and the lake is inspected. This piece of water is about twelve miles long by two miles broad, and the colouring of the water itself is a deep dark blue, of the kind familiarly known as "Reckitts." Good fishing can be obtained here, the record catch being a forty-five pound trout, hooked and landed by a fortunate angler last year.

After tea the party is driven home along a rough mountain road at a spanking pace, the distance of nine miles being accomplished in forty minutes.

Chapter 2

July 29th to August 8th

Banff to Skagway. Laggan. The Summit. Down Kicking Horse Pass on the Cow-Catcher. Field. Palliser. The Selkirks. Golden. Glacier House. Albert Canyon. Revelstoke. North Bend. Vancouver. H.M.S. *Warspite*. Victoria. Mount Baker Hotel. The Parliament Buildings. Union Club Dinner. On board the D.G.S. *Quadra*. Active Pass. Alert Bay. Fort Rupert. Queen Charlotte's Sound. Bella Bella. Perrin's Anchorage. Klemtoo Narrows. Metlah Catlah. In Alaskan waters. Tongass. Steamer Bay. Chatham Straits. The Lynn Canal.

Sunday, July 29th

We leave Banff this morning at nine A.M., on a special train which is to take us slowly through the most beautiful portions of the Rocky Mountains.

At Laggan[1] Her Excellency insists upon mounting the cow-catcher, in front of the engine, the Private Secretary and Aide-de-Camp taking their place on either side of her, while the Superintendent of the line finds a precarious seat upon the only other unoccupied portion of the platform. The Comptroller absolutely declines to be one of the party, having stated last night that he saw no charms in such a method of travelling, and being unwilling to retract this statement.

The Comptroller invariably refuses to entertain any gener-

[1] Lake Louise Station. The name was changed in 1916.

ally accepted view, and, as everybody is unanimous in advising him to have a ride on the cow-catcher, as being a thing well worth doing, he resolutely declines to do so. When we suggest that it is a good opportunity, which should not be missed, he snorts loudly and says that one can do just the same thing, only better, on Mount Vesuvius or up the Rigi. No doubt, were he at either of these two places, he would use the same argument and refer with a similar snort to the Rockies. In this way he would end by seeing neither, and is laying up for himself a miserable old age, full of remorse and heavy with lost opportunities.

The feeling of sitting in front of the engine is always exhilarating, and, at times, almost thrilling, and it is certainly more exciting than travelling under the seat, a procedure for which the Comptroller declares a distinct partiality and preference.

After passing the Summit, at about eleven A.M., where we see the Great Divide and the waters can be noticed flowing in two different and opposite directions within a distance of a few yards, we come to the famous Kicking Horse Pass. Here the grade is sometimes as much as four and a half in one hundred, and the sensation of descending this precipice is singularly startling. At intervals we notice switches, by means of which the train can be turned up the mountain side, in case of accident. On approaching any of these the engineer, if he is confident of having his train under proper control, whistles four times, when the man on duty turns the switch and allows the train to proceed down the main line; if this signal is not given the switch is left untouched and the train turns up a steep incline and eventually stops, of its own volition, in conformity with the laws of gravitation. The scenery all along this route is perfectly magnificent, and it is almost impossible to resist the temptation of taking photographs every two minutes.

The mountain sides are covered with tall pink flowers, named "fireweeds," and which are supposed to flourish wherever a forest fire has left its mark. In this way Nature attempts to make some compensation for the havoc caused by the constant conflagrations which are so prevalent all over this part of the country.

At Field we leave the cow-catcher, and retire to discuss luncheon in the more comfortable diningroom of the car.

On reaching Palliser the Comptroller is induced to pocket his pride and accompany His Excellency and Aide-de-Camp to their old seat in front of the locomotive, the Private Secretary, in the meanwhile, climbing up into the cab of the engine, from which we subsequently see a grimy head appear at intervals.

Soon after this we catch sight of the great range of Selkirks, and their luxuriant appearance comes as a welcome relief to the eye after the stony ruggedness of the Rockies.

The Selkirks are well wooded, gloriously green and rich looking, and the forests with which they are clothed literally sparkle with wild flowers of every kind. The traveller never ceases to wonder at the monument of engineering which the

Canadian Pacific Railway is continually presenting to his aston-
ished eyes. Canyons have to be crossed, masses of mountain-
side tunnelled, and differences of level contended against and
overcome, in a manner that must inevitably win the deepest
admiration.

At Stony Creek we come to a bridge three hundred and ten
feet high, crossing a gully three hundred and fifty feet broad,
and similar structures, many of them built of wooden trestles
only, mark the path of this wonderful stretch of railroad.

Golden comes into sight at about two P.M., when we return
once more to the car, except the Private Secretary, who has
become quite the stoker, has broken his eyeglass and is placidly
smoking one of the engine driver's cigars. He eventually
appears, towards teatime, but his condition is such as to pre-
clude the possibility of his entering the diningroom until he has
had a Turkish bath, or at least a rub down with a wet towel.

At Glacier House there is a stop of one and a half hours for
tea. The Comptroller and Aide-de-Camp, being young and
energetic, discover a Swiss guide who bears an extraordinary
resemblance to Mr. Ivan Caryll, the well-known Chef d'Orchestra at the Gaiety Theatre (London), and politely request him to
take them by the hand and lead them to the Glacier, in order
that they may cool their heated brows against its frigid bosom.

The guide at once produces two mountain ponies, of uncertain age, whose chief characteristics appear to be pachyderma-
tous hides and a great disinclination to work of any kind, and
the expedition starts forth. (Happy thought of the Comptroller's: "A quartet, conducted by Ivan Caryll.")

Travellers intending to visit the Glacier on the ponies provided are urgently recommended to possess themselves of
some sort of goad similar to the one which Louis Stevenson, in
his famous "Travels with a Donkey," used to such advantage
upon the faithful "Modestine." The Comptroller, after endeavouring, by threat and blow, to urge his steed out of a slow walk,
and failing dismally in his attempts, christens the animal "Mus-
tapha Pasha," it being, as he explained, "indolent but with a
certain amount of character." The Aide-de-Camp, whose temper is getting shorter every moment, surnames his beast "Ab-
dul the Damned," that being the only name that efficiently

expresses his feelings. Ivan Caryll breaks his baton almost at once by the rigorous methods of his conducting.

On arriving at the Glacier's foot it is possible to walk inside the enormous mass of clear blue ice and look up at heaven through cracks which are thirty feet high or more. From the top of the Glacier one can look down one hundred and twenty feet into the fissures of solid ice below, and the effect of all these views is cooling, if nothing else.

On the return of the explorers they discover the Private Secretary moping mournfully upon the station platform. After his late experiences of equitation he had not dared so soon to take his seat in a saddle, and so had been left behind, to brood upon his misfortune and the tender state of his epidermis.

The party once more mounts the cow-catcher and the journey is continued. At one point a long tunnel has to be passed through and the Comptroller and Aide-de-Camp, who, after some minutes of total darkness, have become green with terror and are holding on to the engine like grim death, experience a shock which proves almost fatal. This takes the shape of a bucket or two of water, let down upon their heads in the darkness, from the roof of the tunnel, at a moment when such a douche is least expected. The Comptroller's terror allows him, however, to ask loudly "What the douche is this?" and, with a gasp of joy, they presently emerge from the obscurity, and the remainder of the journey passes without incident.

At seven P.M. we stop at the Albert Canyon, a deep gulch with steep precipitous sides. It seems so narrow that one would think it easy to throw a stone across from one bank to the other, but it is almost impossible to do so, and much time and trouble is spent hurling every conceivable missile into space, all of which drop fatuously into the stream, some hundred and seventy-five feet below.

Revelstoke is reached in time for dinner, and here the platform is crowded with mosquitoes and babies. One of the latter mounts the car, holding out a small bunch of flowers as an offering of welcome. When however the critical moment arrives for presenting this bouquet to Her Excellency, he (she or it) becomes very loth to part with the precious flowers, and a

compromise is eventually effected by which she (he or it) shall
keep half of them for itself (himself or herself).

July 30th

We wake at North Bend at eight A.M., and soon the Fraser
River claims our attention, and we follow its circuitous course
for most of the day.

At eleven A.M. the train is boarded by a representative from a
Vancouver paper, who desires an interview. His visit is not
successful, but this fact does not deter him from expressing an
intention of publishing an imaginary interview all the same.

Vancouver[2] is reached at one P.M. and the usual address of
welcome is presented by the Mayor.

In the afternoon His Worship takes the party for a drive
round Stanley Park, where the wonderful big trees, surnamed
"British Columbia toothpicks" are to be seen. One of these the
Aide-de-Camp measures as being twenty paces round the
trunk, and consequently some seventeen feet in diameter.

Their Excellencies and Aide-de-Camp go on board H.M.S.
Warspite (Captain Walker) in time for dinner, and there they
pass the night, in the comfortable quarters of the Admiral.

[2] "It is wonderful to see the strides the country has made since I visited it in
the autumn of '85 with Lansdowne—Winnipeg has become a very fine city—
magnificent streets and asphalt roads—while the city of Vancouver now
some 25,000 population—did not exist when I was here—its site had not
even been cleared of its enormous forest trees—it has since that been built
and burned down once and built up again, till now it is already a beautiful
town with a great future before it, and its public park with its large trees,
some of them must be 15 to 20 ft. in diameter, is worth coming here to see—
It is curious how far in advance the cities of the West are to those of the
East of Canada in many ways. In the West beautiful houses, well kept gardens and fine roads, whilst Ottawa the Capitol [sic] is an example of all that
is untidy and ill kept, the road to Govnt. House from the town so bad it is a
work of danger to drive over it—and Montreal in many respects nearly as
bad." (Letter of Lord Minto to Arthur Elliot, July 31, 1900. Public Archives
of Canada.)

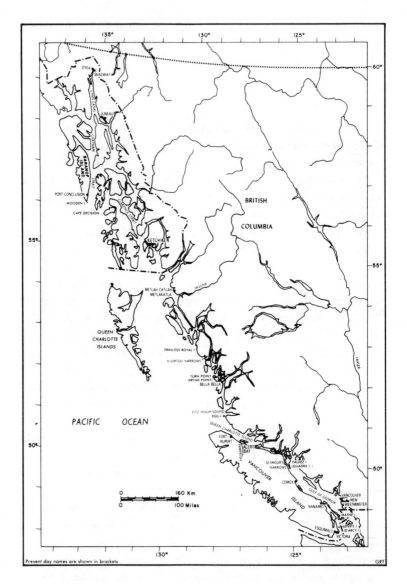

Present day names are shown in brackets

After dinner two members of the ship's band, both Italians, give a little concert on deck, playing violin, guitar and mandoline in a way that causes general admiration and is very soothing to the digestion.

Meanwhile the Comptroller and Private Secretary have dined early on shore and set off in search of adventure, which

they discover in the shape of a seventh rate Music Hall, where the entertainment is only one degree better than the liquor, and where both are altogether beyond criticism. They return sadly to the car Victoria, intending to make an early start next morning, at four o'clock, in the Dominion Government Steamship *Quadra*, which is to take them to Victoria.

July 31st

While the Private Secretary and Comptroller are wending their way across the ocean, at break of dawn, on board the *Quadra*, Their Excellencies and the Aide-de-Camp sleep peacefully upon the *Warspite*.

The Aide-de-Camp is woke up at five A.M. by the conversation of the midshipmen, whose hammocks are hung outside his cabin door. He hears the advisability of waking him up at such an early hour discussed, but, fortunately, the suggestion is rejected as savouring of inhospitality, and he is able to rise, in his

own good time, and consume an excellent breakfast in the Ward Room, at eight-thirty A.M., while the ship is being got under way.

At two P.M. the sad news of the death of His Royal Highness the Duke of Edinburgh[3] is signalled by the Destroyer *Virago*, which has come out from Victoria for the purpose. It is at once gathered that all the plans for Their Excellencies' reception and for the decoration of Victoria must be given up.

Rear Admiral Beaumont comes on board when this city is reached, and the ship proceeds to Esquimalt, where the party disembark on to the *Quadra* and are taken back to Victoria. A short drive takes them to the Mount Baker Hotel (Oak Bay) which they are to make their headquarters for the next few days.[4]

---

[3] H.R.H. Prince Alfred, second son of Queen Victoria.

[4] "Polly [Lady Minto] and the children are living at a very nice house we have taken from a Captn. Clive Wolley ... and self, Harry, the Comptroller and Sladen are at the Oak Bay Hotel... ." (Lord Minto's Diary, National Library of Scotland.)

The view from the Hotel windows is delightful. In the distance the low pinecovered hills reflect their purple shadows in the quiet waters of the bay, while, in the foreground, groups of tiny rockbound islands line the sunny shore. The weather is of the kind to which one is accustomed in the country in England during the summer-time. A bright sun shines warmly down, but there is always a touch of cold in the morning wind, and a bite in the evening air. The grass is everywhere much burnt up, and the scrub-oaks, which give to the bay its name, would be improved and freshened by a little rain. In the town, however, the gardens are everywhere bright with flowers, grown and tended in a way which is unknown in Eastern Canada, and the roads, though deep in dust, are lined with broom, flashing in places a yellow blossom against its shadowy green.

We lunch with Sir Henri Joly de Lotbiniere, the popular and charming Lieutenant Governor of British Columbia, and, after luncheon, are taken to a tennis tournament, where we watch several of the leading players exhibiting all the prowess in the game for which this Province is famed.

In the evening the Comptroller, Private Secretary and Aide-de-Camp take a holiday, dine early, and express their intention of going into the city and "seeing life."

At eight P.M. they start out, to board the nearest tramcar, but are forced to wait half an hour before such a means of conveyance turns up. After being carried about a mile and a half towards their goal they are told to change cars, and wait another twenty minutes before the next train arrives to take them on. In this car the lights have for some reason or other been extinguished, and they rush blindly along, at the rate of at least two miles an hour, with much bell ringing and many stoppages, until they reach their destination, the main street of the city, at about nine-thirty P.M. Thus a distance of two miles has taken one and a half hours in the accomplishment.

The "Savoy Theatre," with its gleaming advertisement, lures them in to a performance which cannot even be called third-class with veracity, and which can have few attractions to anyone outside of a lunatic asylum. The attentions of the ladies on

the stage to the Private Secretary become so marked as to attract general comment, and, as their evident admiration and affection for him remain entirely unreciprocated, the Comptroller and Aide-de-Camp think it best to lead him out of harm's way before any difficulties arise.

Not wishing to trust again to the vagaries of so ill-managed an electric car system, the revellers bargain with a genial cabman, who undertakes to convey them to the Hotel for $2, where they are soon seeking the well-earned slumber which early rising and a day at sea demand.

August 2nd

The air is colder today and the distant horizon is clouded with the smoke from forest fires on the American coast, where, through a veil of blue mist, the Olympian Mountains lift their snowy peaks into the skies.

In the morning the Vice-Regal party is taken for a drive round the city. An opium manufactory is first of all visited, where the genial Chinese proprietor shows forth the mysteries of the trade. The smell of opium is sickly, but not altogether unpleasant, and the Aide-de-Camp is on the verge of becoming addicted to the habit, as a means of passing the time, but, in consideration for his many friends, refrains.

Next the Fire Department is reached, where a display is to be given by the brigade. At an agreed alarm signal all the stable doors fly open and horses canter out of their stalls and place themselves in front of their various engines; the harness, which has been hanging over their heads, is released and falls onto their backs, numerous firemen slide down through the roof by means of steel poles, and, in a moment, the engines, horsecarts and fire escapes[5] are galloping up the street to an imaginary fire. Water is pumped freely over the road, the surrounding houses and the harmless passersby, men throw themselves with some natural trepidation from high ladders into a net held below, and a most praiseworthy exhibition of skill, efficiency and alacrity, is given by all concerned. The fire department of this small Western town can certainly compare more than favourably with that of many of the big provincial cities in England.

The next objects of interest are the Parliament Buildings, where the Legislative Assembly of the Province meet to "make history." This handsome block was erected at a cost of one million dollars, all of which, as they will tell you with pride, was spent upon the object for which it was voted. The plans were designed by a young English architect,[6] and the whole materials, stone, wood and workmanship were produced, contracted for and made, in British Columbia. A small museum is attached to the Buildings, where has been gathered together a collection of all the animals, birds, fish, butterflies, and geological specimens, etc. of the Province. This gallery is well worth a visit, for the collection, though small, is in its way complete, and affords much of interest and instruction to the intelligent observer.

[5] In England a "fire escape" is a ladder truck.
[6] Francis Mawson Rattenbury (1867–1935), who had come to Vancouver less than a month before the contest for the Parliament Buildings. He was also the architect for the Empress Hotel.

With the exception of the Aide-de-Camp the whole party lunch on board H.M.S. *Warspite*, and the Comptroller goes for a cruise on Torpedo Boat No. 39. On the strength of this feat he obtains permission to dine out in the town with a mysterious cousin, and returns to the Hotel, very fatigued, at about two A.M. When questioned the next day as to his movements he maintains a fitting and dignified silence which ill becomes so naturally frank a man.

August 3rd

This morning His Excellency and the Private Secretary start off to visit the forts at Esquimalt, and, on their return, the latter maintains the deadliest secrecy (combined with the most profuse ignorance) as to what he saw there.

The Aide-de-Camp, having partaken of too much iced water on the previous evening at a cheery dinner given him by the Private Secretary, remains in bed till a late hour, and passes the rest of the day in an armchair, where he excites all the sympathy and interest attached to youthful convalescence.

Everybody else is busy preparing for the journey of the morrow, the Comptroller buying furniture and laying in stores, the Private Secretary packing his eyeglass, and the remainder of the party fitting and trying on mosquito netting.

We have all been much worried, during our stay in Victoria, by the motto of British Columbia, *Splendor sine occasu*, which is to be seen in many conspicuous positions in the various Government offices, etc. This legend is extremely puzzling, even to such a gifted Latin scholar as the Aide-de-Camp, and various unsuccessful attempts are made to construe it. The Private Secretary says at once, with the assertiveness of incapacity, that such a task is simplicity itself, and translates it as follows: *splendor:* "display"; *sine:* "is the sign"; *occasu:* "of an occasion." He is hastily urged to reflect that such a translation is the sign of crass ignorance, if not of mental imbecility, and stands temporarily reproved, but unabashed. The remainder of the party put their brains to the task and evolve the following results: *Splendor sine occasu*, according to His Excellency, "Splendor without demoralization"; according to Her Excellency, "Pride without a fall." The Comptroller thinks that it must mean "Glorious only on occasions," while the Aide-de-Camp prefers to translate it "Splendor without any occasion for it." It is only after consulting with the Lieutenant Governor and several of the Ministers that we are able to arrive at the real translation, "Radiance without setting."

This evening His Excellency is the guest of honour at a dinner given to him by the Union Club. The banquet is short, the speeches shorter, and, by midnight, the whole party are sleeping sweetly in their several beds and dreaming of the journey of fifteen hundred miles to Dawson City upon which they will embark on the morrow.

August 4th

After a morning spent at the Jubilee Hospital, the final preparations for the voyage are made, and, at five P.M., the party embark on the Dominion Government Steamship *Quadra* (Captain Walbran)[7] which has been elegantly fitted up for their reception.

The *Quadra* is a vessel of some six hundred tons (registered tonnage), drawing thirteen feet of water, and capable of making about twelve knots an hour, a rate of speed which, with a favourable tide and in clear weather, she is soon achieving, as, on a North Westerly course, she steams rapidly out of the bay, among the numerous small islands which line the coast of North America.

The Private Secretary has already assumed a completely nautical air and attire, and, wearing an old pilot jacket, and with a telescope under his arm, he struts about the bridge, with his legs wide apart and his hat cocked rakishly over his left eye. "Ha Ha," he says, as he sniffs the breeze, "the smell of the salt

---

[7] John T. Walbran was present when the Government Steamer *Quadra* was built at Paisley, Scotland, and except for a few months he commanded the *Quadra* from 1891 to 1903, engaged in the lighthouse, buoy, and fishery service of British Columbia. He was the author of *British Columbia Coast Names 1592–1906*.

sea foam is in my nostrils!" and it is pleasant to know that Nature has provided sufficient room in that organ for a good supply of the article which he appears to relish so.

At about six P.M. we pass the Leper's Island,[8] where the unfortunate sufferers from a horrible disease are dumped down by the Dominion authorities and left to make their living as they please. They are visited once a month by a Board of Health Officer, and provisions are sent to them at intervals, but they are never allowed to leave the Island, this fact eliciting from the Comptroller a misquotation to the effect that "the lepers cannot change their spots."

At eight P.M. we drop anchor in Miner's Bay, in Active Pass, within view of Mayne Island which derives its name from the first Lieutenant of the *Plumper*.

After an excellent dinner, at which the Captain, by his brilliant conversation, proves himself to be at once a literateur and an earnest student of and devotee at the shrine of Nelson, we seek our cabins. Silence, broken only by the Comptroller's strident snoring, broods over the sleeping vessel. A watery moon peers out above the trees, eyeing with some suspicion the unaccustomed craft, and only the soothing murmur of the breeze, ruffling the face of the waters, breaks the peace and quiet of the first night at sea.[9]

Sunday, August 5th

We are awakened by the throbbing of the engines and the pattering of rain upon the portholes. The *Quadra* gets under way at six A.M., in the cold grey light of a showery morning.

There is a big fixed bath in the Aide-de-Camp's cabin, and, at an early hour, the Private Secretary and Comptroller insist on disporting themselves therein, at the same time splashing water all over the floor and walls of the cabin, and using the

[8] D'Arcy Island.

[9] "We were to have sailed on Sunday, but in deference to the narrow minded wish of the Bishop of B.C. managed to sail on Saty. afternoon August 4th." (Lord Minto's Diary, National Library of Scotland.)

folded clothes of the Aide-de-Camp as a suitable spot in which to lay their soap and sponges, while they stand, with wet feet placed impartially upon his boots and socks, and dry themselves violently on his bath-towel.

At nine A.M., after the ship's muster roll has been read over and answered to by the men, a little religious service is held in the saloon; two or three short but pointful prayers of praise, supplication and thanksgiving, are read, and the service, which would only lose by augmenting or amplification, is brought to a close in about five minutes.

By ten o'clock the clouds have lifted and the sun shines brightly down upon the calm waters of the Gulf of Georgia.

After breakfast, the Private Secretary, who has resumed his position upon the bridge, sees a whale on the port bow and is much elated. The animal, however, turns out to be only a "black fish," a small species of whale, and, while the Private Secretary is watching its evolutions with polite interest, it takes an early opportunity of blowing rudely in his face, and, after a series of somersaults, disappears with a final defiant wave of its enormous tail beneath the surface.

On our port side the coast of Vancouver Island is draped in mist and smoke, from the frequent forest fires which are to be met with at every point, while, to starboard, islands of every size and shape, thickly clad with trees, their undulating slopes covered with rocks, present to the eye a rugged and inhospitable appearance, picturesque but not offering many attractions to the would-be resident.

At noon the Three Sisters are passed, a trio of barren rocks situated in the very middle of the bay, uninhabited save by seagulls and the inmates of the little lighthouse which stands whitely out upon the largest of these small islets.

In the afternoon the Comptroller discovers a glorious haven from wind and sun. He collects books and cushions and ensconces himself in the steamlaunch which is slung on the *Quadra*'s deck. This sheltered spot is, however, shortly afterwards observed by the Private Secretary and Aide-de-Camp who, with their natural generosity, insist upon sharing its seclusion with the Comptroller. This place is hereafter christened the "Smoking Room," and becomes a very popular resort.

A little later we pass some Indian villages, with their crests erected on totem poles outside the doors of their huts, and, about five P.M., the *Quadra* steams through Seymour's Narrows, a small channel connecting the main land of Vancouver Island with Valdez Island.[10]

There is a gorgeous sunset this evening. Heavy white masses of clouds rest low upon the hilltops, like banks of cotton wool, and the brilliant orange glow of the sky gleams through them, turning to crimson glory on the mountain sides.

At eleven P.M. the *Quadra* comes to anchor in Alert Bay, where the United States Revenue Cutter *Grant* is also lying for the night. It is only a couple of years ago that this locality was the scene of cannibalism, when, on the occasion of an Indian function of some sort, in which a performance of the "Hamata-a" dance took a prominent part, the body of a girl, who had been dead for some time, was made use of for culinary purposes.

When this unpleasant incident reached the ears of the authorities they caused those of the Indians who had partaken of so unsavoury a meal to be seized and taken to Vancouver to trial, but, owing to some technical flaw in the drawing up of the prosecution, they were acquitted.

August 6th

By seven A.M. we are under steam and the *Quadra* is soon threading her way through a multitude of small islands, frightening gulls and wild duck from their customarily undisturbed feeding places.

The Private Secretary and Comptroller invade the Aide-de-Camp's cabin at the customary bathing hour and these "human porpoises" perform their usual "marvellous splashing act" upon the floor until hunger prompts them to dress for breakfast.

At nine A.M. we see Fort Rupert[11] on our port bow; an old Hudson's Bay Company's post, now inhabited by Indians, who,

[10] Now Quadra Island. The name was changed in 1903.
[11] Founded by the Hudson's Bay Company on North Vancouver Island in 1849.

according to the Captain, are very evil men. The sum of their wickedness, however, appears to be that they resolutely decline to allow any missionaries to live with or near them, a crime which cannot fail to excite a grain of sympathy in the sable heart of the Comptroller.

Cone Islands come in sight an hour later, diminutive, and, as their name betrays, conical-shaped heaps of tree-grown rocks, standing in splendid isolation: undesirable, uninviting and cheerless. The Private Secretary says that he wouldn't like to be "macarooned" on one of these; another such remark and he will be!

At about ten-thirty the *Quadra* steams through Christie's Pass, so called after the Navigating Lieutenant of H.M.S. *Sparrow Hawk*, and the blue Pacific Ocean is in sight.

As Queen Charlotte's Sound is entered a heavy swell makes itself felt, in a manner more forcible than agreeable. The *Quadra* has a reputation for rolling, and she certainly does it justice. The Aide-de-Camp is the first to succumb, and, with a hurried excuse, he leaves the deck and seeks the seclusion of his cabin, where he spends the remainder of the morning, looking, as he subsequently explains, at the lovely view from his porthole.

We pass Egg Island, with its spick and span light-house, at one o'clock, and, by two-thirty P.M., the vessel has entered Fitz Hugh Sound, a piece of water which was originally called Sir John Middleton Sound,[12] but afterwards renamed. The peaceful calm that ensues induces all on board to partake of a post-poned lunch with unnatural avidity.

The first sea-lions are observed today, and, among other curious creatures of the deep, a "thrasher" or "whale killer" is encountered, an animal whose rude practice it is to leap out of the water and descend with a paralyzing shock upon its victim's back, a method of attack that is at once disconcerting and un-pleasant.

At five-thirty the Private Secretary reports "Pointer's Island Lighthouse abeam," and Her Excellency proceeds to photo-

[12] Named Fitz Hugh Sound by Captain Hanna in 1786, called Sir Charles Middleton's Sound by Captain Duncan in 1788 and again Fitz Hugh Sound by Captain Vancouver in 1792.

graph it, a picture being required for engraving on the Admiralty Charts.

At six-thirty we pass the large settlement of the "Bella Bella" Indians, once a wild, warlike race, up to any devilry, now Christianized, missionarized, and consequently peaceful and up to nothing. On the other side of the channel we see their burial ground, a series of small houses, with windows all complete, in which they lay the bodies of their dead, and outside which they erect the totems bearing the family crest of the deceased; a somewhat gruesome method of interment, truly. There used to be a Hudson's Bay post[13] at Bella Bella in 1833, but it was subsequently relinquished and sold.

A little later, at Turn Point,[14] where another of the many neat little lonely lighthouses is situated, the channel broadens, the scenery opens out, and we get a glorious view of distant snowpeaked hills. The nearer slopes present a singularly porcupine-like appearance, where the tall white branchless trunks of the dead trees prick their heads out above the maze of dark green foliage of the living. As far as the eye can reach there is nothing but an endless aggregation of trees in all stages of life, death, and after; flourishing, dying and decaying. Saplings struggling up through the surrounding branches to get a glimpse of the sun; sturdy fullgrown firs, standing strong and straight on their own ground: miserable dying monarchs, pale with age, helplessly leaning for support upon their more youthful neighbours; and so the tale goes on, with a succession of trees more in number than the hairs of one's head, very many more assuredly than the hairs on the cranium of the Private Secretary.

At eight P.M. we lay up for the night in Perrin's anchorage, a bay named after the present Bishop of Columbia, and, shortly after dinner, the party sets forth in the ship's boat, armed with fishing-line and rifle, in search of sport.

Her Excellency and the Comptroller, accompanied by the Second Engineer, set their course towards the Ivory Island lighthouse, and, having baited their lines with decomposed fish

[13] Fort McLoughlin.
[14] Changed to Dryad Point in 1901.

sit patiently and wait for cod. Their expectant ruminations are brought to an abrupt close by the sudden discovery that Her Excellency's feet are under water, and that the boat is leaking fast. The cod are for the moment forgotten, and, while the Second Engineer bails madly with his hat, the oars are resumed and the boat is rowed swiftly back to the ship.

Meanwhile His Excellency, the Captain, Private Secretary and Aide-de-Camp, armed to the teeth, make their way up the quiet waters of Blair Inlet, a distance of about a mile and a half, and there, after disembarking and dismissing the boat, the keen sportsmen conceal themselves in the long wet grass and wait patiently for the possible approach of a misguided deer.

The sun is gradually setting, colouring the low distant hills with a crimson and yellow haze, very similar to the golden sunset splendour of an evening in Egypt. Silence reigns supreme, save for the splash of the oars from the receding boat and the hushing whisper of the warm breeze tenderly stirring the pine tops. A little mountain stream hard by rushes with effortless flow towards the silent bay, muttering low to itself and grumbling at the stones that vainly strive to dispute its passage.

No deer, however, come to test the sportsmen's skill, and, after an unsuccessful wait of half-an-hour or so, the boat is hailed and the party makes its way back to the *Quadra*.

A glass of whiskey toddy closes the day satisfactorily, and by midnight, sleep, the Great Consoler, has once more taken possession of the ship.

August 7th

At eight A.M. this morning the *Quadra* passes through the Klemtoo Narrows, a passage which is only about eighty yards in width. It is here possible to throw a potato, and for the matter of that an onion, from the bridge of the ship, on to the shore on either side. This recreation pleases the Private Secretary so greatly that we are in some danger of living on half rations of vegetables for the remainder of the trip, owing to the reckless manner in which he wastes the missiles with which Nature, and the Steward, have so thoughtfully provided him.

The mountains on either side rise sheer and steep out of the water, rearing their snowcapped summits high above the heavy clouds that rest upon their tree-clad slopes. The scenery much resembles that of the Norwegian fjords, and, as we coast along the eastern side of Princess Royal Island, eagles can here and there be seen sitting on dead branches by the water's edge.

It begins to rain after lunch, but His Excellency and the Aide-de-Camp, undaunted by unfavourable climatic conditions, get out their rifles and practice at the occasional wildfowl which are swimming about near the distant island shores.

Towards evening the weather grows colder and the rain sets in heavily from the north. The Private Secretary, smoking his thirteenth pipe, is lying in a somnolent condition in the Chart Room; the Aide-de-Camp indulging in his twenty-fifth cigarette, is settling himself to sleep in the "Smoking Room," and the Comptroller is lighting the fourth of the Aide-de-Camp's cigars, with one of the Private Secretary's matches, preparatory to seeking a few moments repose in the seclusion of his cabin.

The scenery is rapidly growing monotonous. Nothing but trees of the same size, covering hills of the same height, rising from islands of the same appearance. But, at about six-thirty P.M., we reach the mouth of the Skeena River, where the channel broadens out, and one's eye is attracted by the distant view of low grey ranges of mistbound hills, swathed in shrouds of thin grey cloud under a dead grey sky. In the neighbourhood of the Skeena River, at certain seasons of the year, it rains perpetually. Owing to the peculiar climatic conditions, the Indians who reside here refuse to believe in the occurrence of the original Flood, in which an individual of the name of Noah so distinguished himself, because, as they truly say, it frequently pours for forty days and forty nights in their own district and they are none of them one whit the worse.

At eight P.M. we anchor at Metlah Catlah,[15] on the mainland of Caledonia, a distance of five hundred and eight miles from Victoria. A score of years ago Metlah Catlah was a large and flourishing village; sawmills and canneries existed and the Indian inhabitants lived here in plenty, affluence and peace. This

[15] Metlakatla. In his diary Lord Minto uses the same spelling as Graham.

happy condition of theirs was solely due to the efforts of a certain Mr. Duncan, a lay volunteer missionary, who guided the footsteps of his flock with a firm but kindly hand and viewed their broadening education with the clear eye of guide, philosopher and friend.

Here he built a huge wooden church, in which were held religious services in conformity with the ritual of the Church of England; here he erected a guesthouse, where the itinerant redman was sure of a welcome, and where the traveller could obtain board and lodging for as long as he cared to stay in the village.

Some fifteen years ago however, the Church Missionary Society, looking with fatherly eye upon this Western settlement, discovered, with horror and amazement, that Mr. Duncan was unordained, and Oh! the flutterings of righteous indignation that arose in the dovecots of the Zenana societies in Bermondsey and Little Puddlington-by-the-Sea!

Aghast at this discovery of unorthodoxy, the authorities at home implored the good Mr. Duncan to take holy orders at once. He, worthy soul, no doubt for his own very excellent reasons, firmly but politely declined. The Church Missionary Society thereupon appointed Mr. Ridley, an able English Divine, to the Bishopric of Caledonia, and he at once took up his quarters at Metlah Catlah.

Mr. Duncan seeing that there was no room in one place for two men of equal ability, and working in their different ways to attain similar ends, gathered together his belongings and left the country.

He subsequently settled in Alaska, where he founded the new Metlah Catlah, whither nearly the whole of his original flock followed their trusted friend, deserting home, house and work to join the unorthodox lay pastor who believed that Christianity could be preached to the heathen, as well as practised among them, without undergoing the ceremony of ordination.

This is the sad story which the stranger will be told, if he enquires the cause of the desertion and gradual death of the once prosperous village of Metlah Catlah, but it is only fair to state that we who heard the account had no opportunity of corroborating these facts, nor of hearing, on the other side of the question, the argument which the Church Missionary Society could no doubt bring forward in defence of their incomprehensible actions.

It is enough to know that, by the secession of Mr. Duncan, an able and excellent philanthropist has been lost to Canada, and that, whatever may be the rights or wrongs of the religious controversy which has contrived to change a flourishing settlement into a half empty decaying shell, the result must seem most deplorable to the mind of the educated churchman, most puzzling to the logic of the simple Indian, and altogether unlikely to foster or further the advancement of "propagation" of Christianity in foreign parts.

Rightly or wrongly one's sympathies lean heavily towards the zealous but unordained lay worker, ousted from the scene of his labours, after successfully bearing the heat and burden of the day, before he can reap the harvest which he has so plentifully sown; inevitably one's admiration rests upon the strong-willed Christian, whose personal magnetism is such as to induce his flock of converts to unhesitatingly "forsake all and follow him," a procedure which must necessarily entail a great personal sacrifice to the average Indian, whose affection and attachment to his "Iktahs," or household goods, and his "Illahie," as he calls his country, cannot be over-estimated.

It is impossible, however, to help pitying the formally consecrated and eminently orthodox prelate, lord of a bishopric whose headquarters consist of a practically deserted village, where the empty factories look down with sightless but reproachful eyes upon the big cathedral, once filled to overflowing by a flood of willing worshippers, now sparsely attended by a small and for the most part infantile congregation, and where the wreck of the once crowded guesthouse stands inhospitable and tenantless. "What a Site for a See!" says the Comptroller, as he views the semi-inhabited village, whither he has rowed in an open boat to pay his respects to the Bishop, who receives him with welcome hospitality and entertains him royally at the Palace for an hour or two.

The Comptroller is greatly impressed with His Lordship's charms, and, further, has the privilege of being introduced to a

number of English lady missionaries, (the "Seven Gadarene
Virgins" he calls them, thereby showing his complete ignorance of Holy Writ), who sit at the Bishop's feet in the various
attitudes of unctuous adoration common to ladies in their position.

It is curious to note that the many women workers, who, like
these, have forsaken the thrilling joys of existence in an English
suburb for the satisfaction of ministering to the spiritual wants
of the "poor benighted heathen," invariably regard their
earthly chief with feelings in which awe, worship and romance
are about equally commingled.

August 8th

Up anchor at six A.M. of a bright calm morning, and at about
half past eight, we pass the Lord Rock, and Alaskan waters are
reached. Later, Angle Point, on Bold Island, comes into view
abeam, and, by one P.M., we are steaming through Tongass
Narrows, a passage about two hundred yards wide bounded by
low grass-clad banks richly lined with a yellow rim of drifting
seaweed.

Soon after this the little village of Tongass, commonly called
Ketchiken, comes into sight, a sunny settlement of wooden
houses, nestling among the hills, down by the water's edge. A
mail steamer lies at her wharf as we pass, the Stars and Stripes
fly bravely out over the local revenue office, while, high above
the other houses, a tiny red roof stands picturesquely out
against the rich green background of surrounding woods. In
the distance we catch sight of the United States Revenue Cutter
Albatross heading northwards in our own course, but we fail to
overtake her.

An uneventful afternoon slips by, as we steam swiftly through
the dancing sunlit waters of the broad channel known as Clar-
ence Strait.

After tea a friendly porpoise comes alongside and follows
the boat, in a playful, flippant manner, for about two miles. It
does not appear to be the least afraid of human beings, and,
even when the Private Secretary puts his head over the ship's

side and gazes at it through his eyeglass, expresses no alarm. Subsequently, however, it refuses to take a biscuit out of the Comptroller's hand, and, shortly afterwards, disappears, never to be seen again.

Tonight we anchor in Steamer Bay, where the United States Revenue Cutter *Columbia* pays us a fleeting visit. There must be something particularly suspicious about our appearance to necessitate the presence of these numerous Government boats which seem to haunt our course at every turn, and the Aide-de-Camp begins to wonder which of the many crimes of his youthful but lurid past has been suddenly brought to the light of day.

After dinner we enter the boats and proceed for a moonlight row. The "Gilded Staff" land at an open place on the shore of an Island hard by, intending to go for a good leg-stretching walk, but this plan of theirs has to be given up, owing to the dense impenetrable nature of the jungle, through which they make their way with difficulty for a distance of some thirty yards. Resigning themselves to fate they sit upon a fallen log, smoke the Aide-de-Camp's cigarettes and discuss the question of possible marooning.

The whole forest in which they find themselves is thickly strewn with fallen trees, interlaced and interwoven in every direction, while, overhead, the dense branches twine together, forming a gloomy curtain which veils the moon and further darkens the surrounding maze of shadows. Over every inch of ground and even on the trees themselves there grows a thick carpet of heavy moss or lichen, spongy and soft to the footstep. Not a sound breaks the stillness, and no sign of animal life of any kind is to be observed.

A Robinson Crusoe on this wild Island would find it hard indeed to make a living, for, though the natural growth of yielding moss would serve as a most comfortable bed, it is a great question whether this provision of Nature would be equally satisfactory when regarded as the staple food to be procured upon the Island. The Aide-de-Camp possesses a gold safety-pin, which, as he suggests, could be used as a fish-hook, with which to catch soles; the Private Secretary has a cigar cutter, which could soon be converted, or so he avers, into trolling tackle, suitable for the capture of the wily salmon; the Comptroller has some cigars, which, as all agree, if boiled for some hours in a bucket of rain water over a slow fire, would make an unpleasant but no doubt sustaining vegetable soup. It is to be supposed that berries grow somewhere upon the Island and that clams of some description line the seashore with their nests, but the thoughts of the effect of a perpetual diet of those two commodities upon the civilized digestion are enough to make a strong man weep.

The Aide-de-Camp and the Comptroller both state emphatically that, were they wrecked upon this lonely beach, and left desolate for any length of time, they would certainly have no hesitation in making an end of themselves in the cleanest and most convenient manner. The Private Secretary is inexpressibly shocked at this resolve of theirs, saying that such a proceeding would be very wrong indeed; but they hasten to assure him that it would be only when all hope had been given up, and after they had already killed and eaten the Private Secretary, that they would dream of drawing their own more useful lives to a close.

On returning to the *Quadra*, fishing lines are produced, baited with huge slabs of malodorous meat and let down over the ship's side into the vasty deep. Fishing in this manner is continued for about an hour, the bag at the end of the night's sport being as follows: one halibut, one dog-fish (returned to his native element as being unfit for human food) and one sole. The latter animal is a rare fish in Canada, at any rate in Eastern Canada, and, as we gloat over our victim with watery mouths, thoughts of bread crumbs and lemons flit across our minds and we promise ourselves a glorious breakfast on the morrow.

August 9th

Alas how easily things go wrong! "The best laid schemes of mice and men gang aft agley."

The little band of travellers assembles at the matutinal breakfast-table today with unaccustomed punctuality, only to find, with feelings of disappointment almost too deep for tears, that the sole of last night's capture is, after all, nothing but a species of flounder, which, in the process of cooking, has become a soft unappetizing conglomeration of bones and fat!

It is a heavy heart indeed that prompts the trembling hand towards the safer contents of the bacon dish; it is a teardimmed eye that measures out a portion of the homely omelette! It is a voice shaken by sobs and choked with manly emotion that calls a blessing upon the morning meal.

At about one P.M. we round Cape Decision,[16] and, in a little less than an hour, sight Port Conclusion.[17] Here it was that Vancouver, the explorer, brought his famous survey to a final successful close, and, as he left the port, one of his sailors, a man called Wooden, fell overboard and was drowned, giving, by this accident, his name to the little island situated at the mouth of the bay.

We are soon steaming, with a strong breeze astern, through Chatham Straits, where the *Quadra* has another opportunity of which she speedily avails herself, of giving an exhibition of her powers of rolling.

As the afternoon advances the hills that line the Western side of our passage grow more and more bare and rocky in appearance, while the snow upon their slopes and summits increases in quantity every hour, occasionally a small green glacier may be seen laboriously pushing its way towards the sea, struggling down some steep mountain gully. The base of the hills is clothed with a thick grey mist, through which their red brown sides rise ruggedly to the cool and frozen heights above.

As we are resting on deck, after the effort of partaking of five o'clock tea and cake, a loud snort is heard at our elbow, and, of a sudden, three small whales push three large bodies out of the churning water, within ten yards of the vessel's side, and blow three separate times at us derisively through three ill-mannered pairs of nostrils. At one moment we are afraid that their extreme proximity and apparent familiarity may prove embarrassing, but fortunately, and with unconscious tact, they decline our pressing invitation to come on board, and

---

[16] Southern tip of Kuiu Island.
[17] Near the south end of Baranof Island.

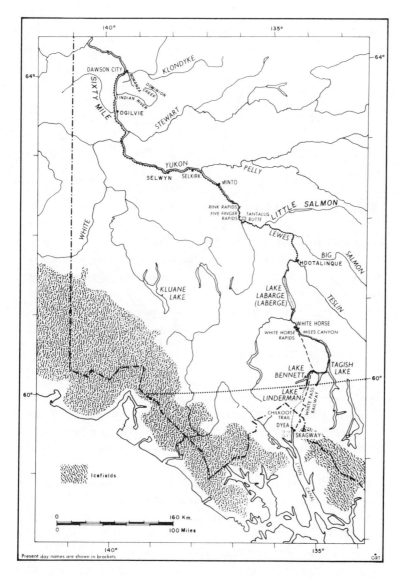

the happy trio are gradually left snorting and blowing in our wake.

Tonight we do not intend to anchor, but shall run at half speed all night, passing through the famous Lynn Canal, which has caused so much international argument and heartburning, and expect to arrive at Skagway tomorrow morning.

Chapter 3

August 9th to August 13th

Skagway to Dawson. Skagway and Dyea. "Soapy Smith." The 24th
U.S. Infantry. The White Pass and Yukon Railway. Dead Horse Trail. The
Summit. Bennett. Caribou. White Horse. "Stikene Bill." On board s.s. *Sybil.*
Jack Dalton. The Yukon River. Woodstacks. Scows. "Five Fingers." The
Rink Rapids. Selkirk and its cemeteries. Some notes on recent fiction.

August 10th

We wake this morning opposite the little settlement of Homes
Mission, and it is not far from here that the celebrated Dalton
Trail commences, the trail by which so many earnest seekers
after gold have found their way to Dawson, after days of weary
journeying.

Soon after we steam into Taiyai Inlet, a narrow channel, in
places over two hundred fathoms deep, with steep sides sparsely
clad with small trees, here and there tinged to a warm autumnal
red. To the west glaciers appear in great numbers and in every
variety of size. At about nine A.M. we sight Dyea, (which signifies
in Indian "the carrying place") ahead of us, and presently, as we
turn a bend of the channel, Skagway itself, the goal of our sea
journey, comes into view.

Skagway has now completely cut out Dyea, and the latter is
practically dead, inhabited only by a few Indians and a deserted storekeeper. The *Quadra* comes to anchor in the bay,
and, after bidding a temporary farewell to our comfortable

quarters on board, we step ashore at about eleven A.M. at Skagway.

It is as interesting as curious to think of the extraordinary mushroom growth of this town, which, not so long ago, was a mere settlement of tents and log cabins. It was only in 1898 that Skagway was in the hands of the notorious "Soapy Smith," a desperado of the worst kind, who completely terrorized the town, and, with his gang of equally repulsive ruffians, waylaid the harmless miner returning with his hard-earned gains from the Yukon, held him up, and relieved him of a large percentage, if not all, of his treasure.

The United States town marshall, the only representative of law and order in the place, was himself one of Soapy Smith's crew, and consequently it can easily be understood that the average citizen could obtain but little redress from his wrongs at the hands of this villain.

To further prevent the United States Government from taking any steps against him, for at one time, such was his notoriety that he feared they might send a ship up to Skagway to hamper his misdoings, he recruited and drilled four hundred men, armed them with repeating rifles and offered them to President McKinley to help fight the Spaniards.

At last, however, he went beyond the bounds of even his own lawlessness, and, on the occasion of a particularly bad piece of highway robbery, the whole respectable portion of the town rose against him, and it was determined to exterminate the desperado and his unattractive clan.

Mass meetings were held all over the settlement, but Soapy Smith, who knew the danger of allowing a mob to collect courage from its numbers, kept going the rounds, with some score of his own armed ruffians, and, somewhat after the manner of a London policeman, dispersed each meeting before it had time to gather boldness enough to make up its mind to any drastic course of action.

A small meeting of this kind was being held on the wharf, and, to prevent interruption, two of its members, a man named Read and a little Irishman, were posted, on the look-out, at the entrance of the wharf.

In a short time up comes our friend Soapy Smith, with about

ten of his "boys," to where these two were on guard. "What the thunder do you think you're doing here?" says Smith, or words to that effect, and at the same time clubs his rifle and raises it over his head, with the intention of striking Read with the butt and upon a tender part of the cranium. Read, with the instincts of self-defence strong upon him, seizes the rifle in his hand, a short struggle ensues, and, in a moment, the muzzle of the Winchester is within an inch of the centre of Read's body, while he, poor man, has drawn his revolver and holds it close to a corresponding portion of Smith's anatomy. The next instant, with a sound like the explosion of a fire-cracker, both men are busy pumping lead into each other, and, to the horror of the watching crowd, a few seconds sees them fall bleeding to the earth, Smith in a dying condition, Read mortally wounded and fated to die of blood poisoning within three days.

After the occurrence of this tragedy the members of the meeting, which it was Smith's intention to break up, stand waiting in some dismay for the next move on the part of Soapy's conspirators. These men are all armed to the teeth and consequently have the unarmed crowd upon the wharf at their mercy. Slowly they begin to advance upon them, but the little Irishman, who was originally on guard with the luckless Read, grasping the danger of the situation, seizes the rifle from Smith's gradually stiffening grasp and holds the advancing party at bay.

As each desperado comes to the front he finds this little man's rifle pointed in an unpleasantly suggestive way at the centre of his waistcoat, and gradually a sort of panic seems to seize the group of ruffians, and, with one accord, they turn and run for their lives.

At once the cowering crowd, of a sudden grown bold at the sight of their enemies in full flight, develop, as is the manner of crowds, the feelings and methods of a pack of bloodhounds. "Get your rifles!" they shout, and rush wildly in pursuit of the retreating remainder of Soapy's band of fugitive miscreants. The scene of pandemonium during the remainder of the night in camp can be easily imagined.

Within a fortnight everyone of Smith's men was captured, and, for three whole days, thirty-five of them were kept in a small wooden house, undergoing their trial before the Vigilance Committee.

Day and night a mob of some six hundred persons, thirsting for blood, howled round the scene of the trial, and it was only by a vote of seventeen to fifteen that the Vigilance Committee decided to hand the criminals over to authorized justice instead of letting them go free to the mob who were so anxiously awaiting their revenge.

This was the end of Soapy Smith and his band, all of whom got sentences ranging from death to imprisonment, sentences which they richly deserved.

The population of Skagway is now somewhere about two thousand. It is the recognized starting place for the gold fields of Alaska, and is growing rapidly and flourishing more and more every day, as the constant influx of would-be millionaires increases.

This little settlement has been the scene of many a hopeful undertaking, many a disappointing failure. It has been the witness to many a well-planned scheme ending in despairing tragedy, many a thoughtless enterprise crowned with the glory of success.

On the shore here, not so long ago, there was to be seen a curious conveyance, resembling a sternwheel paddle boat turned into an automobile. The hopeful inventor designed this extraordinary carriage with the object of crossing the Chilkoot Pass in comfort. The wheels of this amphibious-looking contrivance were inlaid with spikes, a comfortable cabin was situated in the stern, next to the little gasoline engine, and the proprietor was confident that, by such means, he would be able, in a short time, to run a kind of omnibus service to Dawson, and thereby save mankind in general from the hardships of the trail and at the same time line his own pockets with the gold of grateful travellers. Needless to say his invention got no further than the beach of Skagway, where it proved a source of much amazement to many but of no revenue to the owner.

This morning, at about noon, we visit the barracks of the 24th United States Infantry, who compose the garrison of Skagway, and are much impressed by the smartness and physique of these black soldiers, though we cannot help pitying the fate of any troops destined to be quartered in this outlandish place.

In the afternoon our party is taken charge of by Mr. Graves, the President of the White Pass and Yukon Railway, and, in a special train kindly provided for our comfort, we start away from Skagway, at about two-thirty P.M.

The White Pass Railway is another marvel of modern engineering. The original surveys were only made in 1898, in an icebound, precipitous, impossible country, where almost unsurmountable natural obstacles were to be met with at every step, and yet, in July 1899, the first train was able to run along a great portion of the now completed line. The difficulties of labour and construction were tremendous. During the great stampede to Atlin, a year ago, most of the men employed to work upon the line left in a single night, and, out of a staff of twenty-five hundred men, only seven hundred remained to continue the work. All the steel rails had to be brought from Oregon by sea, all the timber for sleepers had to be imported, and, owing to the Spanish-American War, it was almost impossible to charter freight steamers for the purpose. Now, however, in spite of all these combinations of difficulties, the railway is completed to White Horse, and stands prominently out, in the history of railroad-making, a monument of enterprise, ingenuity and pluck.

Shortly after leaving Skagway we pass the Dead Horse Trail, which derives its name from the appalling number of horses that died, on the roadside, attempting to reach Bennett by this route. The inexperienced greenhorn, coming out in search of gold, would buy a horse at Skagway, load him up with every conceivable article, except forage, and start off on the trail with a light heart. Soon the unfortunate quadruped, tired out by the weight of its load, the bad state of the track and the absence of food, would fall exhausted by the wayside and be left to die. Most horses perished in this way, though many broke their legs among the boulders which strew some parts of the trail. It was impossible for the next arrivals to pass the place where the first horse had broken down, except by walking over his dead body, and, in a short time, the road was nothing but a groove worn across an amorphous mass of innumerable and, in a short time, unsavoury carcases.

At the end of a single season thirty-five hundred dead horses were counted in a distance of three miles, and hundreds of half-starved animals would be always turning up in Skagway, to prowl about the streets looking for food, to occasionally obtain a meal from some charitable resident, and, when slightly re-covered from their weakness, to be reclaimed by brutal owners and once more started off upon the fatal trail.

This state of things got to be so bad that at last a Society for the Prevention of Cruelty to Animals was started in Skagway, and, although it had no legal authority whatever, it has man-aged to thrive upon the consciousness that the great consensus of public opinion was ready to back up its actions.

At half-past four we arrive at The Summit, twenty-eight hun-dred and seventy feet above the level of the sea. Here the boun-dary line between Canada and the United States is marked by two flags, the Union Jack and the Stars and Stripes floating bravely out some ten paces distant from one another. Here too, as in the case at the Summit of the Rockies, the water can be seen flowing in absolutely opposite directions; so that two sticks, thrown into the streams at this point, would float, the one fourteen miles to the Pacific, and the other twenty-two hundred miles to the Bhering Sea.

A little later we come to Octopus Lake, which casts great snake-like arms across the countryside, and, after passing Log Cabin, now a mere collection of tents, we cross over to the Chilkoot Range and see the famous Chilkoot Trail in the dis-tance.

This was one of the many roads to Dawson. It started from Dyea, crossed the much-written-of Chilkoot Pass, which, from all accounts, is not nearly so alarming as one has been led to suppose, and finally brought the traveller to the shore of Lake Linderman, where he could go by boat the whole way to Dawson.

Bennett is reached at five-thirty P.M., and our little party is welcomed to the place by the presence at the station of two highland pipers, in correct costume, who play appropriate music as the train draws up at the platform. On the shores of

Lake Bennett we see numerous scows being built; large flatbottomed boats suitable for the transportation of cattle to Atlin or Dawson. There is no longer any service of steamers between Bennett and Dawson, as the new railway is well able to cope with all passenger traffic.

We are descending once more to the land of trees, but, throughout the whole country, one is never able to see any tree with the slightest pretensions to size. The ground is frozen so hard in the winter that it never gets a chance to thaw out, and the roots of the trees, after descending for six inches or so into the ground, reach a perfect bedrock of hard icy soil throughout which they cannot pierce.

On uprooting a tree in this country, a very easy thing to do, by the way, the roots will be found to be perfectly flat, within a very few inches of the surface, and this reason is sufficient to account for the death from lack of sustenance of all trees when they reach a certain age and height.

It is curious to note that, in this vicinity, there is practically no wind at all, whereas at Skagway a gale is generally blowing every afternoon; and there is a local saying here to the effect that it is possible to carry a naked lighted candle from Caribou to Dawson without any danger of its being extinguished.

At Caribou, which is our next stopping place, we are met by an escort of North West Mounted Police, under Superintendent Primrose. There is a sandbar here, across the water, over which, at certain seasons of the year, the scows have to "portage." Here too is the narrow piece of shallow water across which the caribou used to pass in great herds, and which is now known as "Caribou Crossing."

Late this evening we pass within distant view of Miles Canyon and the White Horse Rapids, but are not close enough to see either properly, and at about nine P.M. we arrive at White Horse, where Inspector Wood, of the North West Mounted Police, is waiting to receive us.

The railway only arrived here on June 8th of this year, and yet, in two months, a mushroom city of wood and canvas has sprung up, with a population of between four hundred and five hundred inhabitants, and a Board of Trade, whose members shortly appear and present an address to His Excellency.

Tonight the Comptroller and Aide-de-Camp, together with the two officers of the North West Mounted Police and Mr. Graves, make a tour of inspection in the town of White Horse. A dancing saloon is first visited, where numerous games of chance, "faro," "black jack," "roulette," etc. are in full swing, and where a number of singularly unattractive ladies seem very anxious for the visitors to join the mazy dance in their company, or at any rate, to stand them a drink at the adjacent bar.

The night is brought to a close at a further saloon where a quantity of intolerably vitriolic whiskey is consumed, and where acquaintance is made with "Stikene Bill," the foreman of the White Pass Railway. This gentleman is a great character in his own rough uneducated way, a man who believes in feeding his men and horses as well as he works them, who believes in working himself harder than either, and who has the proud reputation of thoroughly earning the (to the English mind) amazing salary of £100 a month.

Before the railway was completed, passengers wishing to go to Bennett were forced to do the latter part of the journey in horse waggons provided by the Company. The following is a copy of the free pass upon this line of transportation issued by the Company and believed to be the handwork of "Stikene Bill."

Red Line Transportation Company.

Pass _____ subject to conditions on back hereof until Dec. 31st, 1899 unless otherwise ordered.

Conditions.

No. ——— This pass is not transferable, must be signed in ink or blood by the holder, and the person thereby accepting and using it assumes all risk of accident and damage to person and baggage. The holder must be ready to "mush on" at the crack of the driver's whip. "Four Crown Scotch" and "Concha de Regalias" carried as side arms, subject to inspection and may be tested by the officials of the road or their duly authorized representatives. Passengers falling into the mud must first find themselves and then remove the soil from their garments, as the Red Line Transportation Company does not own the country and the authorities are not giving it to "chechacos," (i.e. "tender feet"). No passenger allowed to make any remarks if the horses climb a tree, and, if the sled drops through the ice, each one must retain his seat until the bottom of the Lake is reached, when all are expected to get out and walk ashore. The holder hereof may gaze upon the mountain scenery or may absorb the Italian sunsets, and, if specially desirous, may be permitted to watch the gleaming Northern Lights. If the passenger has but one lung he will have permission to inhale the fresh air to full capacity of said lung, but no bellows will be allowed.

I accept the above conditions.

Signed ——————————————.

The expression "mush on," here used, means nothing more than "walk!" "Mush" is the word with which the drivers of the dog sleighs encourage their teams to progress, and the term is supposed to be derived from the French word "marchons" which has thus been corrupted by the untutored savage of the Arctic regions.

Tonight we all sleep on board the s.s. *Sybil*, a large and comfortable vessel upon which we are to make the remainder of our journey to Dawson City. Mr. Graves also accompanies us, and the two officers and escort of North West Mounted Police are in attendance, to keep a fatherly eye upon us until we return to complete civilization.

We turn into our cabins soon after midnight, and with the slumber of wearied innocence, sleep peacefully through the combined noises of the engine employed to manufacture electricity for lighting purposes and the stevedores busily loading the cargo.

August 11th

The steamship *Sybil*, on board of which we find ourselves this morning, is a large "sternwheeler" belonging to the Canadian Development Company.

Her regular service is from White Horse to Dawson, a journey which she has accomplished in forty hours. The force of the current is so strong that, although her speed down stream is occasionally as much as fifteen miles in the hour, she can only attain to four miles per hour on the return journey up stream.

The Private Secretary, as usual, gets up first this morning,
and has the good luck to meet and be introduced to the notorious Jack Dalton, the owner and maker of the Dalton Trail.
This well-known character is a man of poor education; in
appearance he is short and rather dapper, with steely blue eyes
and a fair curling moustache. Although under forty years of
age he is one of the best known, best-feared men in this country; is a dead shot, possesses absolutely indomitable pluck and
iron nerve, and is known to have killed at least four men in
self-defence. The Private Secretary is much impressed with his
quiet unassuming manners and doesn't attempt to arouse his
worse side, nor to take any steps to assure himself, by personal
observation, of Mr. Dalton's unerring marksmanship.

At nine A.M. we get under way, and are soon rushing swiftly
down the rapid waters of the Fifty Mile River, the name given
to this portion of the Yukon stream.

70   Upon such a big boat as the *Sybil* the question of navigation
on the Yukon is a most difficult and intricate one. The river
twists and turns at every instant, and its snake-like coils teem
with hidden rocks and sandbanks. Steaming through such
waters requires the services of a most competent Captain and a
most able pilot, and, for these positions of supreme importance, men of great "swift water" experience have to be obtained, men who can read the eddies like an open book and for
whom the swirling currents hold no mysteries.

At times, as we negotiate a ticklish corner, the nose of the
boat seems almost to touch the shore, while the stern swings
out into midstream; in another moment the bow is hurled
round by the force of the current, and the stern-paddlewheel
seems, by the proximity of its convolutions, in danger of scraping the river bank away.

The scenery is unpleasing to the eye; the broad stretches of
undulating country, bare and desolate, which are to be seen on
either hand, resemble the bottom of some monstrous drained
and dried-up lake. Stunted trees grow along the river shores,
which are for the most part of shelving sand, though bright-
ened here and there by a tangle of undergrowth and the pink
colouring of the inevitable fireweed.

The Yukon River, known by many different names at the
various points of its journey, is some twenty-two hundred miles
in length, from source to mouth, and, for a navigable stream, is
perhaps one of the most difficult of navigation in the world.
The shoals and sandbanks are constantly shifting, and, at each
season of the year, the currents change and the channel alters,
in proportion as the waters rise and fall.

Never for a single instant do either the captain or the pilot
leave the wheel, which is kept constantly turning, first one way,
then the other, without cessation.

Towards noon we enter Lake Labarge,[1] where steering is a
comparatively easy matter, and, further on, at Lower Labarge,

---

[1] Shown as "Labarge" on "The Province" Map of the Klondyke, 1897; as
"Le Barge" on The Map of Maps, 1898; and as "Laberge" in *National Geographic Atlas of the World*, 4th ed. (Washington: National Geographic Society,
1975).

we stop at a small post of the North West Mounted Police, where we get our first view of a team of the "huskies," or sleigh dogs, half-wolf half-dog by descent, which are of such inestimable value, in the winter, as a means of transportation over the ice.

As is the case at all the police posts, there is a great collection of these animals here, and one in particular, a beautiful big dog, who is stone blind, attracts our special admiration and pity. The Private Secretary throws him a piece of bread, which falls into the water within a yard of where he is standing, but which the poor brute, owing to his affliction, has much difficulty in finding.

We are soon speeding down Thirty Mile River, one of the most dangerous portions of the Yukon, where many boats and lives have been lost.

Only last summer the s.s. *Domville* broke her back on a sand-

bar in these waters, and was destroyed. Her wrecked remains can still be seen, half sunk in the shallower water by the river bank, where the old ship's watchman keeps an eye upon her from a little log hut which he has built there and over which he has facetiously erected the notice "Domville City. Lots for sale."

Further down we see the spot where the *Florence S.* was wrecked this spring. She ran with some haste upon a rock or bank, and turned completely over, an accident in which three lives were unfortunately lost.

Both these ill-fated vessels were commanded by the same Captain, who has now a similarly responsible position on board the s.s. *Clifford Sifton*, and, as he has lately taken her down to Dawson in eleven days, and, with wonderful politeness, hardly overlooked a single obstacle upon the way, we all make a firm mental resolve to avoid, if possible, travelling by that boat in the future.

At seven P.M. we reach Hootalinque, where the river Teslin flows in, and where are situated the customary police post and a few log cabins, the latter temporarily occupied by passing miners, who are either taking a short rest from their labours or have come down in search of provisions.

A couple of hours later we are at anchor, tied up to the shore, near a woodstack where the *Sybil* can obtain a further supply of fuel; and a glorious full moon is shining serenely down upon the scene.

These woodstacks, which are everywhere to be met with, are run by private individuals, who pitch their small camps at likely places along the river, chop and saw the surrounding timber, and deliver it at the water's edge for the use of the various steamers. When a boat requires fuel she merely has to tie up at one of these diminutive lumber depots and measure off the necessary amount of wood from the numerous stacks that line the bank. It is then put on board by the boat's crew and paid for in ready money by the purser, at the rate of from $8 to $12 a cord. A paternal Government levies a tax of fifty cents on every cord cut by the poor devils who own these wood piles, and, from this source, obtains an annual revenue of about $12,500.

Wood is the only fuel used by the boats on the Yukon, as it is almost impossible to obtain good furnace coal at Dawson, and to carry a supply from White Horse sufficient for the return journey would lead to overloading. The purser on board a big boat like the *Sybil* is provided with $1,500. in cash at the commencement of the round trip, which sum is to be used for the sole purpose of buying wood for the boat, a fact which clearly shows how much fuel is necessary to enable the engines to propel a steamer up the rapid current of this river. It is calculated that the average vessel burns about one cord per hour on the down course, and about one and a half cords per hour on the return trip.

During the journey to Dawson it is almost imperative for boats in these waters to tie up at night, as the passage is so intricate, and the stream so strong and swift, that the slightest mistake would be very perilous; on the return journey, however, the boats usually run night and day, as the consequences of an error in navigation up stream are not naturally so fatal. At times, of course, this difficulty of steering in the dark is happily solved by the presence of perpetual daylight, but just now, the night comes on at about eleven P.M., after which time it is not over safe to venture out into the stream.

Sunday, August 12th

"Grouse shooting begins!" What memories do these three simple words recall! Thoughts of that distant country whose purple heather we have so often trod on previous anniversaries of this day; recollections of the past and of the many happy hours spent on "the hill" upon the "glorious twelfth"; these and a thousand other memories come crowding uninvited into the mind, only to be ruthlessly expelled by the rushing tide of circumstance, and swept away into the distant backwater Regret, to join the choking driftwood of remote impossibilities!

On entering the Lewes River the country grows flatter, the valley opens out and broadens before us, and, as we descend the stream, the shores are more and more thickly covered with small firtrees. The first occurrence of interest to-day is the stranding of a scow, an accident which takes place upon a small shoal of sand to starboard of us. We watch the unfortunate crew wading about in a hopeless, dazed manner round their humble craft, preparatory to unloading her of a large and assorted cargo and attempting once more to float her out into the deeper water.

These scows are very hurriedly built as a rule, of not over-thick timber, and frequently come to grief upon the various sandbars and rocks of which the Yukon River boasts so large a number. As a means of transporting cattle or imperishable goods, such flatbottomed boats are most useful, but they are naturally extremely slow, and cannot be recommended, as a means of conveyance, to anyone to whom time is in the least an object. As it is impossible for scows to attempt the up-stream journey, they are usually sold at Dawson for the value of the wood used in their construction, and can generally fetch a price averaging about one half of their original cost.

Further on, a small row-boat, unskilfully manned by two intrepid oarsmen, gets caught, close to the shore, in the wash of the *Sybil*, and is at once capsized, giving its passengers an invol-

untary bath, which, as the river is principally fed from the
water of melting glaciers, must necessarily be more bracing
than pleasant.

The s.s. *Victorian*, another of the boats belonging to the
Canadian Development Company, comes into sight soon after
this. She is lying up close to the shore, where, owing to the breakdown of her engines, she has been forced, for the present, to
take refuge.

The course of the stream is gradually becoming more and
more snakelike and curling, and, at Thirty-Three Point Woodstack, the curve is so great that the boat's compass shows a turn
of thirty-three points, being more than one complete revolution on that instrument. In the distance we see Tantalus Butte,
a hill which earns its name from the fact that, although it
appears to be close at hand, and is situated, as a matter of fact,
about one and a half miles away, as the crow flies, it is only after
the boat has made fifteen miles, and, in that distance, nearly a
dozen turns, that the long-expected hill is finally reached.

The next object of interest is a coal mine, which has been
lately discovered and is now being actively exploited. Its principal shaft is sunk to a great depth, into the high shelving bank of
the river, and it is believed that, before very long, a useful kind
of good lignite coal will be obtained here in great quantities. In
view of the rapidly decreasing supply of timber, and the inces-
sant demands for fuel in these parts, such a discovery should
prove invaluable.

The coal question is, however, still in an indefinite state, and
although many traces of the mineral have been found along
the river, little progress in its development has been made as
yet. Several mines, however, have been opened up between
Dawson and the mouth of the Yukon, and there is one, about
twenty miles up the Klondyke, which is only just prospected.

Our attention is momentarily withdrawn from the mine by
suddenly finding ourselves running ashore with great rapidity.
By a slight miscalculation, at one of the sharpest turns of the
stream, the bow of the boat is brought with great force into the
bank, in a manner which is a trifle alarming to anyone unaccustomed to travelling by these "swift-water" steamers. Except, however, for a severe mental shock, resulting, in the case

of the Private Secretary, in temporary cardiac failure (which necessitates an immediate dose of alcohol and aerated mineral water), no harm is done by the collision, and, after making a complete revolution upon her own axis, the *Sybil* steams off unharmed, and apparently unabashed, to deeper channels.

The wreck of the s.s. *Reindeer*, which was burnt to the water's edge last year, causes a momentary flutter of excitement, after which we very soon catch sight of the perilous "Five Fingers" and the rapids of the same name foaming at their base.

The Five Fingers, a quintet of large rocks, are situated, like stepping stones, at varying intervals across the stream, and, through these dividing spaces, the water rushes, in a most rude and hasty manner, into the broader channel beyond.

The river steamers have to pass between two of these rocks, through a passage which is only about one hundred feet broad, a feat that was always extremely difficult, and has now been made even more so by official tinkering. Before attempting this passage it used to be necessary to get the boat's head laid exactly straight for the opening, when the chances were all in favour of the current dragging her through in safety. The Government, however, have seen fit to send up an Engineer, to try and improve matters, and he, with amazing cleverness and perception, has blasted away some of the rocks on one side of the channel only, so that the stream is no longer a straight one, and the passage has now to be approached, from the side, at a more than usually difficult angle.

The current here is so strong that the engines have to be reversed, in spite of which accidents are of frequent occurrence. Only a short time ago the s.s. *Lightning* scraped against the rocks in her descent, and, in a moment, the whole of one side of the boat was torn away.

There is a police post at Five Fingers. Here too part of the Dalton Trail debouches, and cattle, who have reached this spot in safety, can be conveyed, for the remainder of the journey to Dawson, in scows.

Five minutes after passing through these rapids we sight the s.s. *Tyrrell*, and Mr. Graves, to whom we owe an everlasting debt of gratitude for his kindness and attentions, and whom as a companion we shall greatly miss, bids us farewell and steps on board this boat, with the intention of returning to White Horse.

Towards five P.M., as we approach the Rink Rapids, we observe a large wooden family-vault type of structure, standing out in all the glory of its painted solitude in the very centre of the river. This is known as "T————'s construction," is so called after the Government Engineer of "Five Fingers" fame, and marks the presence of a hidden rock.

The cynical captains of small craft regard this monument with feelings of scorn tinged with dislike, and, when questioned on the subject, explain their sentiments in no measured terms. Firstly, they aver that the rock indicated by this monstrous erection was so well known to every navigator on the river as not to need marking; secondly, they declare that, whereas in the old time a small boat that got whirled by the current on to this dangerous rock, had a chance, if the water was high, of getting safely over it, any craft that now runs against this tower of Babel cannot avoid meeting with instant destruction.

The skippers who command the larger boats, and who are presumably older and wiser, do not comment at any length upon the handiwork of the well-meaning engineer. So long as the ingenuity of men does not add too greatly to the difficulties already created by Providence they are perfectly satisfied.

At about seven P.M. we reach Minto, a small collection of log cabins, named after the Governor General. Four men have recently been murdered on the trail between this place and Hootchikoo, another similar settlement situated a few miles up the river. This fact alone would seem to imply that the climate of the district is unhealthy for travellers, and must necessarily tend to direct the footsteps of intending residents to other localities.

After passing safely through another of the most difficult and ticklish portions of the river, euphoniously known as Hell's Gate, the *Sybil* eventually arrives at Selkirk at about nine P.M.

Here the intention is, after reloading the boat with fuel, to tie her up for the night. Unfortunately the wood pile to which the *Sybil* is accustomed to look for supplies on such occasions is bare and empty, and she has to turn and steam up the river for some distance before a single cord of the required article can be found.

(Happy thought, which strikes the Private Secretary: "The Lost Cord.")

In the mining districts persons holding licenses are entitled to cut all the timber they may require for mining operations, on their own claims or on vacant Dominion lands. A yearly license to cut timber may be issued to anybody for a bonus of $250 per square mile, no one person to be granted more than five berths of five square miles each. A stumpage of $2 per thousand feet, for cut timber, is also demanded.

The supply of wood along the upper river is fast getting scarce, but, along the lower river, it is practically inexhaustible, though the cordage available bordering the regular steamboat channels is limited and the expense involved advances every succeeding year.

August 13th

Early this morning the Private Secretary goes off, with his gun under his arm and a few cartridges belonging to the Aide-de-Camp in his pocket, with the firm intention of shooting several grouse for breakfast. Soon after landing he steps heavily into a wasp's nest and is kept busy for some time picking the stings out of the various portions of his person, and using language which in his calmer moments he will regret. After a long walk of two or three hours, in the course of which he climbs a hill, which, as an inhabitant of the place assures him and as he naturally likes to believe, is far steeper than the Chilkoot Pass, he returns to the *Sybil* empty-handed, having only had one shot and that without an ultimate result.

After breakfast we all go on shore to admire the beauties of Selkirk, a city that boasts of at least a dozen wooden houses, several cemeteries and an absentee Bishop. The principal occupation of the inhabitants of Selkirk appears to be the burial of deceased Indians; the decoration of tombs is their chief industry, and funerals form their favorite topic of conversation. "Come and see the graves," is the first thing a Selkirk man says

to the stranger who lands at this place, and, in accordance with
the general desire of the residents, we were marched from
cemetery to cemetery in a sort of triumphal funeral procession,
to gloat over the remains of Red Men who had joined their
ancestors in the "happy hunting grounds" of their belief.

These Indian tombs are different from the ones we saw at
Bella Bella and along the sea coast. Here they bury their dead
in the ground and erect small tents, or wooden boxlike structures, over them. These vaults are painted with every shade of
colour and decorated by a variety of crude and cryptic designs.
Sometimes the dead man's property will be buried with him,
and we could see shawls, blankets, and other articles hanging
over the wooden railings of the graves; sometimes a weird
figure is carved at the entrance of the tomb, or a kind of scare-
crow is hung up outside, for the purpose of frightening away
any evil spirits who may be in the vicinity, and for the time
being, out of employment.

Greatly cheered by our visit to the cemeteries we embark
once more, at about eleven o'clock, and the *Sybil* proceeds upon
her journey.

The scenery is as uninteresting as it is unfertile, and the hills
through which we pass, and which are gradually growing
higher and more desolate, seem to produce nothing more
nourishing than sand and sickly looking moss, relieved here
and there by the presence of a plenteous crop of rocks and
boulders.

After luncheon it begins to rain and we are forced to seek
our cabins, there to write long letters home, containing vivid
pictures of the Klondyke as we have seen it described in books.

There must be something about the air of the Yukon which
causes the most upright man, when writing his experience of
the climate of this country, to economise facts to an uncon-
scionable extent. Whereas, in all the accounts that one reads,
he has been led to believe it to be always either bitterly cold or
appallingly hot here, yet, in reality, during the latter part of the
summer, the weather is very similar to that of England, and
residents will assure you that there is no more pleasant and
salubrious climate in which to spend July, August and September.

Then again much has been written about the malarial mosquitoes and other poisonous flies of the Klondyke; how they make sleep impossible, meals uneatable and life unbearable; a state of things which, so reliable inhabitants will tell you, is entirely fictitious and false.

At certain times of the year the mosquitoes appear here in great numbers and are naturally very vicious, and, in the vicinity of swamps or marshy ground, they are often found to be unbearably maddening to man and almost fatal to beasts. Their season, however, is not a very long one, and, by the date on which we find ourselves in the country, these insects do not seem to us to be nearly as bad, nor as numerous, as the pests which we have encountered in Ottawa, or Banff, or at many other points of our journey.

As a proof of the effect of the gilded atmosphere of this portion of the globe there is a place on the old Skagway trail which it has been found necessary to christen Liarsville, and whose inhabitants are perfectly prepared to set up the reputation suggested by such a name.

The humble chronicler of these pages often wonders whether, by disburdening himself of the scruples of a lifetime and giving freer play to a prolific imagination, he could not make this journal far more interesting than he can ever hope to do by consistently sticking to facts, as he is at present doing, in his praiseworthy attempt to describe things as they really are and not as he expected to find them.

The rain continues to fall in dense showers all the afternoon, the outlook is desperately dismal and we are not even to be cheered by being shown the exact spot where the two river-boats, the *Stratton* and the *Willie Irwin*, were locked in an ice-jam last spring and went incontinently to the bottom.

It was our original intention to stop at Selwyn, but, owing to the forgetfulness of the captain, who went to sleep and omitted to warn the pilot of our desire, we passed this settlement without noticing it.

At about seven P.M. we reach Stewart River, with its policemen, its dogs and its log cabins. Each post of the North West Mounted Police is provided with half a dozen sleigh dogs, and the Force possesses more than two hundred and fifty of these animals scattered all over the various districts.

As night draws on the river banks grow steeper and more barren in appearance, until at last we reach Ogilvie, at about ten P.M., where the good ship *Sybil* anchors for the night, confident in her ability to reach our long expected goal, Dawson City, on the morrow, at a reasonable hour of the morning.

Chapter 4

August 14th to August 17th

Dawson City. Dawson. Saloons. A "clean-up" on Bonanza Creek. The
Roads. Nuggets. Expenses. Permits. The Administration of Justice. The
Royalty. "Trade-dust." A visit to the stores. The Departure. General
notes.

August 14th

This morning at ten-thirty A.M. we catch sight of the high hill
overlooking Dawson City, where the white chalky blaze of a
land-slip marks the grave of an Indian village, supposed,
according to ancient legend, to have been buried in a nocturnal
avalanche.

Within half an hour the City itself comes into view, a town of
wooden houses, of every description and size, situated by the
very water's edge, at the base of bare surrounding hills.

To our right the Klondyke River joins its dirty sand-white
waters to those of the Yukon, at a point about a mile above
Dawson, and, looking up the Klondyke valley, we notice the
hundreds of little log cabins, homes of the humble but ever
hopeful miner, which constitute the settlement variously called,
by its inhabitants "Lewestown," by non-residents "Lousetown,"
and by the prouder section of the community "Klondyke City."

A salute of twenty-one guns is fired from the barracks of the
North West Mounted Police as the *Sybil* steams up to the wharf,
and, after the usual presentation of officials and addresses, the

Vice-Regal party, accompanied by Mr. Ogilvie, the Commissioner for the Yukon, is driven to the police barracks, where a comfortable wooden house has been placed at the disposal of the visitors. By a singularly curious coincidence the date of our arrival at Dawson is the fourth anniversary of the discovery of gold in Bonanza Creek by George Carmack, in the summer of 1896, when the great stampede to the gold fields took place.[1]

[1] The date commonly given for Carmack's discovery on Bonanza Creek is August 16th. The following will explain Graham's date of August 14th: By a strange coincidence the 14th of August, the date of the arrival of Lord and Lady Minto in Dawson, was the anniversary of the date on which the first discovery of gold was made in the Klondike district by George Carmack, namely August 14, 1896, or four years ago. This was pointed out to His Lordship by Mr. Wade when reading to him the address of welcome from the Board of Trade. (*Dawson Daily News*, 16 August, 1900)

A little later on in the day, we are driven out in a four-horsed waggon to inspect the beauties or otherwise of the town. Dawson has a population of five thousand souls, and, by adding to this the numerous miners residing on neighbouring creeks, the total number of inhabitants of the district can be roughly assessed at about twenty-five thousand, though, with such a drifting population, no satisfactory estimate can be obtained. Only one third of the inhabitants are British subjects, the great majority being citizens of the United States, with a good sprinkling of Swedes and other aliens.

The Yukon territory is governed by a Council of six,[2]

[2] "I received all the leading men I had time to receive... . Mr. Clement a member of Council & its legal adviser was under arrest when I arrived on an accusation of some corruption & though he was out on bail I naturally saw nothing of him." (Letter of Lord Minto to the Hon. J. Chamberlain August 19, 1900. Public Archives of Canada.)

appointed from Ottawa, to which number, two more, elected by the vote of the people of the territory, have recently been added, and the members of this body have an extremely difficult position to fill, and, with their present limited powers, can never hope to give complete satisfaction to anyone, except perhaps to themselves.

The roadways of the Dawson streets are many of them constructed of saw-dust, the stores and shops appear to be open day and night, the street corners abound in loafers of every description, while the side-walks are lined with dog teams of "huskies," "malamouts" and other humbler specimens of the canine breed, harnessed to every variety of vehicle.

As we approach the confines of the town the chief object that attracts the eye is the immense number of empty tin cans, of every size, which lie in thousands upon all sides of the innumerable log cabins dotted about on the rocky hill slopes. The poorer inhabitants appear to live exclusively upon canned food, and there is surely here a great field open for an enterprising inventor who can put the masses of empty tins, which are thrown away in such quantities, to any practical use. The motto "One people one tongue," much quoted at Dawson, evidently refers to the canned commodity which forms the staple food of the Anglo-Saxons of this City.

In many of the humbler cabins, belonging to men who cannot afford to glaze their windows in the orthodox manner, these apertures are filled with a dozen empty mineral-water bottles, placed, in an upright position, side by side, so as to exclude the air, but, at the same time, to give free access to the sunshine.

This method of using soda water bottles to take the place of the more expensive glass dates back from the time when no miner's hut was thought to be complete unless a bottle of "Pain-Killer" were hanging outside the door, to fill the purpose of a thermometer. When the "Pain-Killer" began to curdle and grow thick it usually meant that the temperature was about thirty degrees below zero, and, at seventy degrees below, the mixture would freeze, intimating to the occupant of the house that it were wiser for him to remain indoors, where he no doubt occupied his leisure time opening tins of canned provisions or indulging (with an eye to future windows) in a bottle of "hootchinoo," the name given to the vitriolic alcohol of the country.

About two miles out of the town we are shown a cemetery, recalling pleasant memories of Selkirk, where the suicides of Dawson are buried in company with the unfortunate wretches who have suffered the extreme penalty of the law, and, further on, we come to a small market garden containing a few vegetables and flowers and quite a fair supply of earth.

The district has for a long time borne a bad name for barrenness and want of fertility, and this diminutive experimental farm is a proof that such a reputation is undeserved. Fruit and vegetables are still, however, worth their weight in gold, the latter luxury being the most common at present.

This evening His Excellency holds a Reception, open to all residents of the male persuasion, which is largely attended. Among those present we notice Mr. Frank Slavin, the pugilist, who is at present combining his original avocation with that of a miner, no doubt with pleasure and profit to himself.

After dinner the Comptroller, Private Secretary and Aide-de-Camp make up their minds to go round the town and visit, in the interests of scientific research, every quarter where instruction or amusement is to be obtained.

In Dawson every third house is a saloon, where drinking, gambling and dancing go on day and night. There are also several music halls, where indifferent performances can be watched from boxes whose chief feature appears to be a total want of privacy from the intrusion of persons of the weaker, and thirstier (but not, in their case, fairer) sex.

After these entertainments the floor of the hall is cleared and the voice of the master of the ceremonies is heard imploring gentlemen to "take your places for the dreamy, mazy, waltz!", when, having induced a sufficient number of the more weak-minded of those present to obtain partners, he orders the band to "let her go" and dancing is kept up until six A.M.

Beyond the payment of a slight fee strangers are not obliged to secure a formal introduction to the lady guests, the latter endeavouring, by the warmth and enthusiasm of their welcome and their complete willingness to fraternise with the most

homely of the opposite sex, to make up for the absolute lack of
personal charms with which Providence has not seen fit to endow them. These ladies get a commission on whatever their
partners drink at the bar, and, when it is remembered that they
can get five dollars on every bottle of champagne (sold at thirty
dollars) it will be seen that their occupation is as lucrative as it is
unalluring.

At about three A.M. the Comptroller was seen performing a
barn dance (in the interests of science), with a sweet creature of
some eighty summers, who was unsuccessfully trying to explain
to him that the tune played by the band was a waltz, a fact of
which he seemed absolutely oblivious.

The Private Secretary was meanwhile pursuing his re-
searches at an adjoining roulette table, where he was so rapidly
assuming the gaunt haggard appearance of the confirmed
gambler that the Aide-de-Camp considered it time to remove
him.

Soon afterwards the three students of life were to be seen
wending their way obliquely to another saloon, where a complete stranger insisted on standing them a large number of
singularly unpleasant drinks.

It is not safe to decline to drink with any men in Dawson, as
such a refusal is taken as a deliberate insult. A warning to this
effect is usually given to strangers, but the question of living up
to such advice entails the making of sacrifices involving consequences which anyone would gladly avoid.

The expense of buying anything at the bar of a saloon is
almost beyond belief. "Wine," i.e. champagne (Jenkins Fils) is,
as has been said before, fifteen dollars the small pint, and the
cheapest drink of mineral water costs fifty cents.

These gambling saloons and dance halls are winked at by the
authorities. The proprietors are regularly brought up in Court
and fined every month, the fines imposed being calculated at
about fifty dollars per man employed and amounting to eight
hundred dollars or so. In this way a revenue of some eighty
thousand dollars is brought in annually, with which to carry on
the expenses of the City.

The proprietors of the saloons etc. come to look upon these
fines merely as a part of their working expenses, a sort of tax to

be taken into consideration when calculating profit and loss, and charge their customers accordingly. Consequently the general public suffers both morally and monetarily, the gambling continues and the man in the street pays the fine.

After a short walk round the suburbs of the city, from Main Street to Paradise Alley, in the course of which the party sees much to give them food for earnest thought, home is reached soon after five A.M. and, for a few brief moments, a short but much-needed rest is indulged in.

August 15th

At ten A.M. this morning the Comptroller, who is suffering from, what is locally termed, a well-developed and protracted jag, the Private Secretary, who appears to be endeavouring to cultivate an unsuccessful skate, and the Aide-de-Camp, who is occasionally observed to be furtively warming his hands on his head, turn up with somewhat guilty expressions to breakfast.

An hour afterwards the whole party, mounted on all Dawson's available saddlehorses, start off for a ride up Bonanza Creek, where it is proposed that they shall be shown over a placer mine,* and where they are expected to arrive in time to see the operation known as a "wash-up."

The ride out, a distance of about nine miles, is over a trail which has evidently never been mended or touched by the hand of man since the Flood, and which is totally unsuitable for any kind of traffic.

Dawson has only one proper road, recently built by the Council, across the Ridge to Dominion Creek, and transportation to the other rich creeks, Bonanza, Eldorado, etc. is, except in winter, extremely difficult. Only a rough trail leads to these claims and even this is invariably in such condition as to make it impossible for any heavily loaded waggon to attempt the journey.

The only bridges across the rivers are toll-bridges, and, as a

---

*A placer mine is one in which the soil is operated and gold extracted by the washing process, as opposed to a quartz mine, where the work is done by crushing.

The Comptroller, Arthur Guise (*left*) and Captain Graham (*centre*).

general rule, the streams have to be crossed by means of fords, which, when the water is high, are not only difficult but also dangerous.

In spite of the fact that the Dominion Government receives every year from the goldfields in royalty, taxes, etc. a sum of not very far from two millions of dollars, or one-tenth of the annual production of the territory, the only money ever voted for the purpose of making or maintaining roads is a paltry fifty thousand dollars, which, at the rate of wages at present prevalent in Dawson, would be barely sufficient to pay for the employment of about one thousand men for five or six days.

The Ridge Road has reduced the expenses of transportation to one-fifth of the original cost, but that a similar route is badly needed on the lower creeks can be easily understood from the fact that, at present, the freight of goods from the City to the Forks costs as much as the freight of the same goods from Victoria to Dawson.

Through fords and into morasses we wade and blunder, over our ears in water, up to our knees in mud, until at last we reach claim "No. 32 below Discovery" where Mr. McGillvray, the Manager, is waiting to show us round, and where a "clean-up" is in the course of preparation.

Owing to the state of the ground in the Yukon, where the soil, at a depth of about two feet below the surface, is always frozen to a solid mass, it is almost impossible to use pick and shovel or even to blast with any successful results. The earth has first of all to be thawed, before it can be worked at all, and, for this purpose, a machine called the "Steamthawer" is used. Long hollow steel thawpoints are driven into the gold-bearing formation, above the bedrock, and, by means of steam, giving a pressure of one hundred pounds to the square inch, the soil is gradually melted and loosened for a distance of about four feet above and three feet below the insertion of the points.

This process enables the paydirt to be shovelled out, carted down and dumped into the large wooden troughs awaiting its reception. A strong stream of water is then allowed to flow through these troughs, washing away all the light useless dirt and only permitting the heavy auriferous particles to sink to the bottom, where they remain, caught in rows of riffles constructed for the purpose.

The contents of the troughs are continually kept moving, until gradually the residue grows less and less, and finally the foundation boards, containing the riffles, are taken out and washed, when the flow of water is stopped and the dry bottom of the troughs is found to be covered with gold dust and small nuggets. This is carefully collected and brushed into a pan, which is then stewed over a stove to remove the moisture.

All fine particles of dust and sand are then ejected with the aid of a pair of bellows and the remainder of the pan-load, constituting the "clean-up," and which to-day is valued at about five thousand dollars, is put into a "poke" or long narrow deer-skin bag, and can be conveniently carried into the town by the fortunate owner.

A slight diversion is caused today by the action of one of the party, who sees fit, in the excitement of the moment, immediately after the completion of the "wash-up," to tread in the pan containing the result of the day's labours. In a moment gold-dust to the value of several thousands of dollars is lying scat-

tered upon the ground, and the task of scraping it together again without losing a fragment of the precious metal causes the worthy foreman some irritation and yet more trouble.

After luncheon the Comptroller and Aide-de-Camp descend privately, with an official accomplice, into a long tunnel where the pay-dirt is being shovelled out, and having filled a pan, commence to wash it out in an adjoining tank, after the primitive method of the humbler placer miner. Their efforts are altogether unsuccessful, and when, after much labour, the dirt is all shaken and washed out of the pan, only the faintest speck of colour, at the very bottom, proclaims the presence of gold to the value of about ten cents.

Meanwhile Her Excellency is being instructed in the use of the "Rocker," a machine suitable for a slightly more advanced method of washing than the panning, and resembling in appearance and facility of working a large infant's cradle.

On the homeward journey we come across an unfortunate man who has started out from Dawson with a pair of magnificent horses, purchased this very morning, one of which has fallen down on the impossible trail and impaled itself fatally on a stake which happened to be situated in the centre of the road. Much sympathy is felt for this sufferer from a type of accident which is only too common just now and which will always be possible so long as no effort is made to give the miners better means of transportation.

At Her Excellency's suggestion a subscription is raised, for the purpose of providing this man with another horse, (an animal which costs about five hundred dollars just now in Dawson), to enable him to carry out a contract which he had just signed for carrying wood, and which, with a single horse, would be impossible.

A small official dinner completes the day's work, and, by midnight, an hour when the remainder of Dawson is beginning to wake up and grow lively, the tired explorers are sleeping soundly in their little cots; the Private Secretary brimming over with experience and wise thoughts and hootch; the Comptroller full of benevolence and "benedictine."

August 16th

The rain is descending in torrents this morning, and, in consequence of the inclemency of the weather, a proposed excursion to the Eldorado mines has to be put off.

This gives us a full morning in which to see Dawson by daylight, having hitherto only been able to judge of her attractions under the glare of her blazing saloons.

To Dawsonites, the question of time and season seems to make no difference. They are so accustomed to months of perpetual night, followed by months of equally everlasting day, that they appear to take little interest in the rising or setting of the sun, and are ready, and even anxious, to stand anybody a drink at any hour of the twenty-four.

The generosity of miners with their nuggets is proverbial, and the stranger is welcomed by the constant remark "Won't you have a nugget with me?" just as in other parts of the world he would be greeted with "Come and have a drink."

Her Excellency has already been loaded with these nuggets by private individuals, and the miners are combining to present her with a large collection on the day of her departure.[3]

It is all the more extraordinary that the inhabitants should be so generous when one considers the enormous price of every article, and especially of liquor, and it is incredible to understand how the residents of Dawson, who do not happen to be millionaires, and there are very few of the latter about just now, can manage to live on limited incomes, with apparently no conception of, or regard for, the value of money.

The days of excessive extravagance are, however, at an end, and, although it is no uncommon thing for a man to lose two thousand dollars at the roulette-table at a single sitting, it is seldom now that one can see a miner hand his poke of gold-dust, containing all his worldly possessions, across the bar of a saloon, and stay there until he has drunk or helped to drink the lot.

Prices which would "flabbergast" men from "the outside," as the rest of the world is called, pass absolutely unnoticed in this city, and, when one realises the expenses of living in Dawson, he can easily understand the residents going away for the summer to Ladysmith (during the seige) for the purpose of economising.

A small wooden house with three or four rooms, suitable for the accommodation of two men, can usually obtain a rental of from one thousand to three thousand dollars per annum.

A room in a respectable hotel costs five dollars per day, and, for this sum, nothing more is provided than a chair, a basin

---

[3] The miners' gift was a miniature golden bucket with a small windlass, pick and shovel, the bucket being filled with gold nuggets. Chosen to make the presentation was Big Alex McDonald, who had come to Dawson City unschooled and poor, but had become very rich and a leading citizen. His fellow miners patiently coached him in a presentation speech in which he was to say that the gift was not being presented for its intrinsic value but as a token of esteem. Alex forgot the words but remembered the idea. Handing the little bucket to Her Excellency he said: "Here tak'it. It's trash." Next day the *Dawson News* reported: "The presentation was made by Mr. Alex McDonald in simple, but eloquent language."

and jug, and a cracked looking-glass, leaning in an intoxicated manner against an angle of the bare wooden walls.

The following items are taken haphazard from the bill of fare of a middle-class restaurant in Dawson, where the excellence of the cooking varies in inverse proportion to the prices,* and the meat is hard enough to provide the dentist, who tactfully resides next door, with plenty of occupation.

Porterhouse Steak	$3.00	(12s./4)
Mutton Chop	1.50	(6/2)
Veal Cutlet	1.50	
(with bread crumbs or gravy 50¢ extra.)		
Two Eggs (any style)	1.50	
Ham and Eggs	1.50	
Ham Omelette (for one person)	2.00	(8s/2d)
Codfish Cakes	1.50	
Lettuce	0.50	(2s/03/4d)
Pork Sausage	1.50	
Plain Cheese	0.50	
Spring Chicken	5.00	(1-0-6 1/2)
Half ditto	3.00	

Extras.

Fried Onions	$0.50	
Tinned Peas	0.50	
Chicken Salad	2.00	
Tea and Coffee – per cup	0.25	(1s/0 1/4d)
Chocolate or Cocoa, do.	0.50	

Champagne, $20 to $30 per bottle, and other liquor in proportion.

After partaking of a meal from this menu the patient may need to visit a doctor, in which case the usual fee for a consultation is $5, and, for a prescription, $10, prices which almost equal those demanded by a firstrate London physician!

The reason for the enormous cost of drink, a necessary luxury in a city where the water is not all that it should be, is not very far to seek.

*Note: ($1.00 in Canadian money is valued at 4s/1 1/4 of English money.)

Although the Yukon is not a "prohibition state," there has been instituted within the territory a system of liquor "permit" which can only be stigmatized as disgraceful. No liquor is allowed to be manufactured in the territory, and, in consequence of this law, all legitimate breweries in Dawson and the District have had to shut down, and the beer which is everywhere for sale in enormous quantities is entirely of American manufacture.

Permits are not issued direct to the saloon-keepers, who pay licenses to sell liquor and should therefore be in a position to be allowed to import the liquor itself, but it is an acknowledged fact that these permits are in the hands of one or two persons, who, by some means or other (it is perhaps better not to enquire too closely) are able to obtain them from Ottawa, and who sell them at largely increased rates to the licenseholders.

It is at present impossible to get a permit, or to sell liquor, except by the grace of these favoured parties, who, it is to be presumed, do not carry on the traffic out of pure love for their fellowmen, and who are, no doubt, not entirely above accepting, in some form or another, a slight reward for their trouble. A system by which favoured speculators can obtain permits denied to the legitimate dealer, and can sell them, or the liquor, at their own price, is not only absolutely unjust to the dealer and costly to the public, but it is an intolerable state of things, which almost constitutes a national scandal and which should not properly exist in any portion of Her Majesty's Colonies.

After luncheon our mounts of yesterday are brought round to the door and we ride out about nine miles along the Ridge Road. This is the only road built by the Council and they are naturally very proud of their achievement. It is of no service to the miners of the big Eldorado, and Bonanza Creeks, but is no doubt of great value to those who hold claims on Dominion Creek, and, at any rate, enables anyone who has the time at his disposal to ride out from Dawson and obtain a magnificent view of the surrounding country and of the Rocky Mountains in the dim distance.

During our eighteen mile ride we have plenty of opportunity and time for the discussion of the many questions of interest and points of difference upon which the officials and miners argue and quarrel without cessation. There is still a feeling abroad that the regulations for the administration of Justice are not all that they might be, though the Department here is at present in the most efficient hands.

Until recently there was only one Judge in the territory, and the Court of Appeal was situated in another Province, but now there are two Judges, and even these are hardly sufficient to undertake the work of satisfying the litigants who are always so numerous in large mining districts.

Owing to the fact that the mining regulations have been changed seven times since they were first drawn up, and that, in consequence of this, there are at present eight different kinds of placer claims recognized, litigation is very frequent, and the settlement of the titles of a good claim will often need two or three surveys and half-a-dozen lawsuits.

Then too miners hardly ever make contracts other than verbal ones and consequently have but poor means of recovering their wages. Even if they sue their employer, and he pleads insolvency, they have at present no right to seize his mine or working plant. The system of carrying appeals in mining cases to the Minister at Ottawa is very unsatisfactory, the difficulty of getting witnesses to attend causes great delay and expense, and it is thought that the Territorial Court could deal with all appeals, with results quicker and better than is the case under the present system.

Miners are birds of passage and cannot wait for months to settle a dispute. Men waiting trial in Dawson would be almost invariably willing to be tried by a Judge in preference to waiting for the empanelment of a jury, and it is generally considered that the appointment of a Magistrate would help to expedite the administration of Justice, which is at present very slow and laborious.

The officers of the North West Mounted Police are, by reason of their office, Justices of the Peace, but their jurisdiction is singularly limited, and they have to refer most cases to the Territorial Courts. Nevertheless, the absence of all lawlessness at Dawson is most remarkable and can only be put down to the wholesome dread with which the old-time crook and evildoer regard the police force.

There is practically none of the crime so prevalent in the big mining camps of California and elsewhere, no weapons are allowed to be carried by the inhabitants, and any breach of the peace is quickly punished by a term of labour at the wood-pile situated in the barrack-yard of the North West Mounted Police.

It is interesting to see the efficiency and utility of this smart body of men, and then to learn that the Dominion Government has but lately refused to grant a permit to supply them with beer for Christmas festivities; an altogether outrageous case when one considers how insufficient is the pay of this invaluable force while quartered at such an expensive place as Dawson. The men are naturally unable to pay the local price for beer ($2.50 per bottle) and are consequently reduced to drinking tea or water. This state of things may please the faddy prohibitionists at Ottawa but cannot do much towards lightening the lot of the overworked constables who practically manage the whole interior economy of Dawson, acting as gaolers, warders, policemen, coroners, soldiers, sheriff's officers, and anything else that is required of them.

The great bone of contention between the inhabitants and the authorities, and the cause of all the bad-feeling, at present running high at Dawson, is the Government royalty, which, it is believed and hoped, is shortly to be removed altogether, or, at any rate, greatly reduced.

This tax, which was primarily fixed at twenty percent, and finally reduced to ten percent, of the gross output of the mines, has had the effect of stopping the development of most of the poorer claims, and of forcing many of the richer mining claims to be operated at a loss.

Whatever royalty is imposed on the gross output of mines must of necessity diminish the extent and area of ground profitable for working, and consequently the number of inhabitants who can find work must be reduced in proportion.

The ease with which the accounts of royalties to be paid to the Government can be falsified is a direct incentive to fraud, and that thousands perjure themselves over this question is obvious from the fact that only $700,000 is paid in royalties on a gross output of seventeen and a half millions, a sum which, even after subtracting the many small outputs exempt from royalties, is totally inadequate.

This tax is practically levied on the cost of all mining plants, as well as on the actual output, wages and working expenses, and it must be remembered that the frozen ground demands the use of steam thawers, the cheapest of which cannot be obtained for less than $1,000.

The general opinion appears to be that the royalty should be reduced or done away with altogether, that an export tax should be substituted, and that a Government Assay Office should be established at Dawson, where the gold could be taken from the miners, and bullion certificates, negotiable and transferable, given them in return.

Among the grievances it is alleged that, although all benches and hillsides on Bonanza and Eldorado creeks were closed against locations by free miners in 1899, and although these districts have never been reopened for the location of placer mining claims, certain parts of these closed portions have been granted, as hydraulic concessions, to large companies at a merely nominal rate. The parts thus closed to the ordinary prospector are, many of them, entirely unfit for any hydraulic working, and it is urged that the companies will end by operating them as ordinary placer mines, to their own great advantage and to the natural indignation of the ordinary miner, who has been kept from working them himself.

On returning from our long ride, most of which is spent trotting furiously down a nine mile descent, we are all so tired that, with the exception of the Comptroller, we are quite prepared to retire to bed at an early hour.

The Comptroller, however, has an appointment in the town at eleven P.M. and is not heard of again until the next morning, when he returns to barracks with his pockets full of peanuts and an absolute lack of all recollection as to where he obtained them.

The only lucid memory he has is of trying to throw a large man of American origin, who had given vent to pro-Boer opinions in an adjoining saloon, into the river. Whether he succeeded in doing this, and, if so, whether the man was drowned or not, cannot be gathered from the fragmentary conversation of our distinguished colleague.

This is our last day at Dawson, and the morning is spent in a visit to the office of the Gold Commissioner, where we see the dust melted down and made into bricks, and where we are shown the different coloured varieties of gold-dust that comes from the different claims.

The recognized local currency of Dawson is "trade-dust," an inferior and less pure quality of gold-dust, and the system of exchange in vogue can hardly fail to be demoralizing to the inhabitants.

A miner can sell his pure gold-dust to the banks at Dawson for about $16.00 or $17.00 per ounce; he can then buy inferior "trade-dust" from them at about $14.25 per ounce, and is allowed to use this as currency in the town, where it is worth $16.00 per ounce. The unfortunate merchant has therefore to take, in payment of a debt of $16.00 or in return for goods whose value is $16.00, dust which is really only worth $14.25, and, in order to get even with this system, he very naturally adds a percentage to the price of his goods, and thus the cost of merchandise is increased.

This system opens the door to every sort of fraud and there are at present in Dawson several men whose sole employment and occupation is to doctor up gold-dust for the trade, a condition of things which could only be avoided by the use of "chechaque" money, i.e. the ordinary currency of "the outside."

Later on in the day we are shown round the three largest stores in Dawson, the North American Trading & Transportation Company, the Alaska Commercial Company, and the Alaska Exploration Company, in whose enormous warehouses almost the entire food and fabric supply of the country is stored for the winter.

Here you can buy wheat at twelve cents the pound; which is about ten times the price paid "on the outside," while hay is twenty cents the pound, a reason for the extreme scarcity of horses in Dawson and for the fact that these animals are usually shot, on the approach of winter, and become food for the dogs which, at that season, take their place.

Owing to the altogether insufficient means of transport from Canadian ports and the far advanced energy and "push" of our neighbours in the States, almost two thirds of the goods imported into Dawson are of American pack and manufacture, and come up the river in large steamers from St. Michaels.

Each of the big companies has its fleet of river boats, consisting of huge sternwheelers, capable of accommodating about two hundred and fifty first class passengers, and making about five trips in the season.

The journey from Dawson to St. Michael's takes about eight days or less, but at least fourteen days are necessary for the return trip up stream, and these boats are so large and heavy that, if they chance to run on a sandbar, it often takes weeks to get them off again.

The price of a first class passage on these steamers is about $70.00 for the down-stream journey and $125.00 for the return trip, while, in the same ratio, freight costs $70.00 to $100.00 per ton.

We are booked to leave Dawson at five P.M. this afternoon, but, owing to a slight breakdown in the engine room of the *Sybil*, we were unable to go aboard till nine P.M., at which hour we embark amid the most enthusiastic demonstration of the assembled populace.

This is in curious contrast to the comparatively cool reception accorded a few days previously on arrival. A population consisting almost entirely of aliens could hardly be expected to grow wildly enthusiastic over the advent of Her Majesty's representative, but the warmth of their cheering on the day of departure gives strong evidence of the popularity gained in so short a time by the personal charm of Their Excellencies, which appeals alike to British subject and American citizen.

So, loaded with good wishes and nuggets, we steam away on the good ship *Sybil*, and, as the darkness deepens over the brilliantly lighted streets, give a last look to the city which we are none of us likely to see again, and to the many friendly faces of those who have entertained us during our stay, we smile a farewell which it is impossible to consider as other than final.

We have seen much during these three last days, and it is to be hoped that we have also learned something, but the time has been a short one in which to obtain very much information upon such an intricate subject as placer-mining, and, at Dawson, the sources from which information may be gained are as biased as they are unreliable.

As has been said before, the City is divided into two camps, the officials and the "kickers," that is to say those who are dissatisfied with the existing state of affairs.

These latter, in whose ranks may be numbered many level-headed business men and as many professional agitators, accuse the officials of being, if not actually venal and corrupt, at any rate absolutely incompetent.

The officials on the other hand declare that all who criticise their methods are either knaves, actuated by the basest motives, or else are merely natural born liars.

It is perhaps possible to steer a clear course between the two extremes and to come to the conclusion that the "kickers" have many real grievances, which, in their efforts to obtain redress, they naturally magnify out of all due proportion; that, in the ranks of officialdom, there are many able men, that there may be some who are incompetent as there certainly are several who are grossly prejudiced; that there is need of much patience, as well as reform, and that neither is likely to be very evident until the Ministry at Ottawa begins to take a little more intelligent interest in the government of this territory.

There are no schools at Dawson, although children are already numerous in the city; there are no roads to the richest creeks, although it is entirely to the advantage of the Government that the miner should have some sort of transportation; and, unless the many obstacles are removed from his path, there will soon be no prospector rich or energetic enough to come into the country and work out, at a loss, the golden treasure it contains.

The authorities at Ottawa do not appear to realize that it is impossible for men residing some five thousand miles away, many of whom never have seen a goldmine, to make regulations suitable for the constitution of a mining camp.

They hardly seem to take any interest in this vast territory, which is larger than either Ontario or Quebec, and twice as large as Great Britain; nor does it ever strike them that some consideration should be shown for the representations of a people which is paying, in customs, royalty etc. one twenty-fifth part of the total gross revenue of the Dominion, and living in a district which, in proportion to the size of its population, is producing a greater revenue than any other part of the British Empire.

The officials at the Capital get their information second-hand, and cannot see for themselves that by harmful regulations, such as one which prevents the relocation of abandoned or lapsed claims, or another which prohibits the prospecting and locating of alternate blocks of ten claims, they are closing the country to the average miner, and allowing a vast expanse of valuable soil to lie fallow and unworked.

Until they take the trouble to look a little closer into the administration of the Yukon Territory, until they have the courtesy to read and reply to the various communications of the officials, and can find patience to listen to the grievances of the "kickers" of that territory, and, above all, until they put a stop to the disgraceful system of "permits" now in vogue, there is no doubt that the general resentment and dissatisfaction, at present felt towards the treatment received from head-quarters, is not likely to grow any less pronounced.

The supply of gold in the mines of the Yukon is apparently inexhaustible, but the supply of patience in the hearts of the inhabitants of that territory shows distinct signs of coming to an end. Unless something is done to make the conditions of life in the district more tolerable, and to prove that, while the gold out-put of the mines is ever in the memory of the Ottawa Government, the population of those mines is not entirely forgotten, there is some likelihood of the one decreasing as fast as the other diminishes, a condition of affairs which will be most painful to the officials of the Treasury Department and of great detriment to the country at large.

This criticism is not levelled at the head of any particular party Government, of any particular creed or way of thinking, so much as at the system of legislation at present existing with reference to matters concerned with the Yukon Territory, a system which is likely to continue to obtain in a country where Parliament is mainly, if not entirely, composed of professional politicians.

With such thoughts as these uppermost in our minds we steam away from Dawson, steering in a southerly direction up the Yukon River towards the settlement of White Horse, where we but lately embarked upon the *Sybil* on our down stream trip to the Klondyke.

PART II

HOMEWARD BOUND

Chapter 1

August *18th to August 31st*

Dawson to Victoria. Back on the s.s. *Sybil*. Our Orchestra. Some
early ideas and much general conversation on the Klondyke. White Horse.
The Rapids and Miles Canyon. Skagway. On board the *Quadra*. Metlah Catlah. The Cannery at Alert Bay. Comox. Nanaimo. Victoria.

August 18th to August 31st

The long journey up stream is very dull and monotonous. One
soon tires of the same range of scenery and the same endless
prospect of curling river, through which the *Sybil* dashes
bravely southwards at the breakneck rate of four miles an
hour.

Soon after starting we are made aware, by a concatenation of
discordant sounds, that a number of ladies and gentlemen on
board have formed themselves into an impromptu orchestra,
and are determined to cheer our otherwise peaceful moments
with singularly unsuccessful attempts at harmony.

This worthy but misguided little band consists of two ladies,
one of whom plays indifferently on the violin while the other
labours more than indifferently at the piano; and the male sex
is represented by a cornet player and a melancholy performer
upon the clarionet, both of whom have cultivated a distinct
prejudice against all recognized laws of synchronism and give
evidence of a strong disinclination towards concord of any
kind. Prayer, entreaties, all are useless, and we sadly make up

our minds to bearing, with all the philosophy at our command, the perpetual aggregation of false notes with which the quiet of the ensuing week is threatened.

After patiently listening, during the whole of one forenoon, to a practice carried out by this quartette, the Comptroller suggests that, perhaps, if all the musicians were to exchange instruments, a better result might possibly be obtained, a suggestion which the performers themselves do not seem to take in the kindly spirit in which it is offered.

The Aide-de-Camp gives it as his unbiased opinion that, if all the members of the band were to drop their instruments of torture overboard, or, better still, (but this is almost too much to hope for) were to fall overboard themselves, day would perhaps be made less hideous, while conversation and correspondence would be momentarily possible.

If one could be permitted to criticise the performance of such an orchestra one might say that there is a distinct lack of "aplomb" and "verve" about their playing and that they certainly need "execution." "They do, indeed," fervently adds the Comptroller, with thoughts of the scaffold uppermost in his mind.

The Private Secretary, after listening intently for seven hours to the excruciating sounds which issue periodically from the saloon, states that, to him, there is always something rather immoral about the violin.

On being questioned he assures us that he doesn't know anything at all about music, his ignorance upon such matters being so great that it is only when some kind friend removes his hat by force that he is ever made aware that "God Save the Queen" is being played. (Cross-examined. *Question:* Have you been drinking? *Answer:* No Sir.) He is strongly urged not to be an ass, and promises to make a more strenuous attempt for the future to overcome his natural tendencies.

"Water, water everywhere, and not a drop to bathe in!" is the Aide-de-Camp's remark, as he kindly hands one of his choicest cigars to the Comptroller and gazes thoughtfully into the muddy stream of the Yukon. Baths are an unknown luxury at Dawson and are naturally unobtainable on board the river steamers, so we must perforce content ourselves with the an-

ticipation of a protracted wash on the *Quadra,* where very shortly we hope to be.

"Now for a smoke!" says the Comptroller, as he throws the half finished cigar out of the Aide-de-Camp's window and lights up an ancient and pestilentially sulphureous pipe of his own, which eventually has the desired effect of driving the orchestra out of the saloon, the musicians departing, amid a cannonade of choking coughs, in search of a purer atmosphere.

"Of two evils choose the lesser," and we are always subsequently left in undisputed possession of the saloon whenever the Comptroller sets fire to his inflammatory pipe.

On arriving at the famous "Five Fingers" the *Sybil* hitches onto a steel hawser, which is fastened to the shore some way up stream, and, with the aid of a steam capstan, tows herself up the rapids. This performance takes nearly half an hour, a period of time which compares curiously with the half minute required for the same passage on the down-stream trip.

Soon after this we pass the s.s. *Zealandian*, stuck on a rock which has pierced a hole in her side, an accident which necessitates the removal of all her cargo before she can be repaired and resume her northward journey; and it is not long before the *Sybil* herself encounters a sandbar, where she remains firmly imbedded for some minutes amid general excitement.

During the long tedious hours on board we spend the time discussing the ideas we have formed upon the gold district, our earlier expectations and final impressions.

It appears that the Private Secretary's juvenile anticipations were not entirely realized. He had from early childhood been led to believe that Dawson was the centre of a golden fairyland, where nuggets grew thick upon the beach and where the genial prospector could fill his hat with the precious metal whenever he felt so disposed.

According to the ideas of the Private Secretary's infancy, all you had to do, in this delightful paradise of gold, was to hire (the merely nominal rent to be paid quarterly in advance) a little log villa, with a verandah and creepers, somewhere near a hill which bore symptoms of producing gold in large quantities.

Then, every morning, before breakfast, you would take a coal-shovel, a garden hoe and a hayrake, and start out "prospecting." After a few minutes of hard digging you came upon a nest of the nuggets which you were seeking and would fill your pockets with the best specimens, taking care to replace the ones you didn't require, and return home in time for breakfast at nine-thirty A.M., or, if you preferred it, for family prayers at nine o'clock.

When the morning meal was concluded and digested you would be off again, with a hatchet, a tin-opener and a small steel tooth-comb, with which to split and scratch suitable looking rocks and extract the gold-dust. Having obtained as much of this as you required for your immediate needs, or as you could persuade your hired man (who also combined the avocations of valet, gardener and head coachman) to carry on his back, you would once more wend your way to the little homestead, where your wife (or, if unmarried, your housekeeper) would by this time have prepared a choice luncheon of onion soup, scrambled brains, damper omelette, hard tack, emergency rations and such other little luxuries as your taste and the state of your finances suggested.

In the afternoon you would clean up, load and full-cock your sixshooter, secrete it in a large pocket situated somewhere about the small of your back, where you couldn't possibly get at it without blowing your legs off, and stroll leisurely into the nearest town, there to change your golden store into coin of the realm at the local bank.

Every week-end you would probably give yourself a holiday, going, by means of the omnibus service, which runs to and from civilization every twenty minutes, to the nearest seaside health resort, there to sit in the rotunda of a fashionable hotel, with your feet on the mantelpiece, while your thoughts wandered comfortably back to the little log villa, where your wife (or, if you were unmarried, your housekeeper) was mending your socks and reading the Sunday service to the children or (if your housekeeper) to the servants.

On Monday morning you would return to work, with some little present in your pocket for your wife (or housekeeper), a patent selfrocking bassinette, say, for the former, or a nice cake of cheap soap for the latter.

After a few weeks of this joyful existence you would naturally become a millionaire, when it was customary to go to England, buy a house in Park Lane, engage a butler who awed and frightened you, a groom-of-the-chambers who looked upon you more in sorrow than in anger, and three powdered footmen who smiled pityingly upon you. Here you could give biweekly musical receptions, at which Calvé, Melba, Coquelin and Paderewski performed (while nobody listened), and could consequently send notices to the newspapers to say that most of the people present at your soiree on "Wednesday evening last" came without receiving invitations.

Your wife (or housekeeper) would, of course, be left behind in the old homestead, where she could no doubt obtain satisfactory and sufficiently accurate information as to your movements by subscribing to a local press-cutting agency, and learn, from the columns of the *World* or *Vanity Fair*, whether you were to be seen "sitting in Hyde Park" after church on Sunday, or had been observed "hurrying westwards in a hansom" on the following Tuesday afternoon.

When the Private Secretary gives free rein to his imagination he takes a great deal of stopping, but, in response to an appealing look on the haggard face of the Comptroller, who has for some time been trying to make himself heard, he at last brings his observations to a close.

The Comptroller, until he visited Dawson, held the view, still shared by a large number of otherwise intelligent people in the outside world to-day, that the Klondyke is a cold, desolate, ice-bound region, where the gold has to be picked out grain by grain from masses of impenetrable volcanic rock, where the desperado and the outlaw abound, where neither life nor property are held sacred, where food is as scarce as whiskey is plentiful, and where only men of herculean physique and rugged constitutions can stand the dangers and privations of existence.

The Aide-de-Camp, however, armed with the wisdom of certainty, pretends never to have had any false illusions or expectations and to have realized all his earlier ideas. *Of course* he knew that Dawson was an ordinary little wooden town, that the climate of the Klondyke, though occasionally severely cold and at times over-poweringly hot, was often mild and pleasant. *Naturally* he was aware that gold was as plentiful there as work; that wages were as high as expenses; that no men of energy, who possessed a pick and shovel, need starve; that every man with capital and enterprise could make enough to live on comfortably; that crime in Dawson was as scarce as good liquor, and that you needn't travel far to find a less attractive spot in which to take a temporary residence.

Some kind person at once suggests Cape Nome, where the smallpox has wrought frightful havoc among the numerous gold prospectors, and this gives the Private Secretary an opportunity to make a remark to the effect that "there's no place like Nome!" Another crime of this sort and our worthy friend will be forced, by an outraged band of fellow-passengers, to give, as they say at the Variety Halls, his "famous impersonation of Jonah!"

We had none of us any idea of the expenses of living in Dawson, but this was very forcibly brought to our notice one morning by a brokendown looking tramp, a regular type of professional beggar, who whiningly assured us that he has had nothing to eat for three days, and implored us for the love of heaven, to give him "fifteen dollars" to "buy a bit of breakfast with!"

There seems to be no golden mean of existence in Dawson, and the young men in business in that City must of necessity choose between the only two practical modes of life possible. Either to keep entirely to themselves, living shut up in their houses, after office hours, with, metaphorically speaking, the blinds down; in which case they probably die insane in a few months; or else to turn night into day, "go the pace" and practically live at the bars and roulette tables of the different saloons; in which case they very shortly die, if one may be permitted to coin such a word, indrunk.

The number of "good young men" who go wrong in Dawson is appalling; there seems to be something in the air, and yet more in the liquor, which conduces to rapid demoralization. Even respectable bank clerks, possessing no redeeming vices, and who were rightly described as being so tame that they would "eat out of one's hand," have been returned to their sorrowing families, after a few months at Dawson, with no occupation left to them but that of living on their debts and no worthier attributes but a taste for indifferent "hootch" and a totally perverted sense of rational enjoyment.

The conversation turning upon the question as to whether money is to be made in any quantities at Dawson by the ordinary business man, the Comptroller says that, if you keep your eye on coal and let gold alone, you will rapidly make an immense fortune beyond the dreams of avarice. The difficulty of this scheme is that there is so little coal to keep an eye on, that all the available portions of this commodity are already being watched with a distinctly jealous optic by other men, who have anticipated the Comptroller's perception by a few years, and that the strain of tearing the eye off chunks of gold for the purpose of glueing it on to chunks of coal is very apt to bring on ophthalmia in its most malignant form.

"Give me $20,000," says the Private Secretary, "and, in twelve months, I undertake to double it for you!" As however no one seems anxious, or even willing, to adopt this unselfish suggestion, and, as the Private Secretary appears to be somewhat vague as to his intended method of duplication, the matter is allowed to drop before the required sum has been deposited into the hands of our hopeful speculator by some confiding philanthropist who is anxious to get rid of a part of his superfluous wealth.

The Aide-de-Camp, with characteristic originality, has a scheme for importing game-cocks into the Yukon, where the time-honoured sport of cockfighting is a very popular one and is only restricted by the rapidly diminishing number of combatants.

His idea is to hire a big hall and give exhibition matches twice a week to crowded houses, the cost of admission being $25.00, so as to make the gathering a fairly select one, and an additional fee of $5.00 being charged for permission to pat the victorious fowl.

At eleven P.M. the *Sybil* reaches White Horse and the Comptroller, Private Secretary, and Aide-de-Camp leave the boat and spend a great part of the night in the local inn, a populous and noisy saloon, where every article of virtue, from the towels to the drinking cups, is marked with the distrustful and rather tactless legend "stolen from the———hotel."

In the morning of August 23rd we bid an affectionate adieu to Captain Cox and the officers of the *Sybil* and take a last lingering farewell look at the steamer which has sheltered us these many days. A particularly affecting parting has taken place between His Excellency and a lady of Scotch extraction who is on board, and who insists on telling him the whole of her past history, including most of the domestic incidents of her singularly long and utterly uninteresting life.

"Ah, my poor dear mother," she is heard to say, "there's a woman for you!" ("Not for me!" His Excellency mutters, beneath his breath.) "Only ninety-seven, and as young as ever! Such a woman for hobbies you never did see! Why I'm sure you'll never guess what my poor mother's present hobby is!" His Excellency chivalrously swallows a yawn, and, with marvellous patience, agrees that he is equally sure he never will. "Ah," she continues triumphantly, "the Queen and all the Royal

Family! That's my mother's hobby! And she only ninety-seven
and as young as ever!"

Finally His Excellency tears himself away from further conversation of this inspiriting kind, and, at about eleven A.M., the
whole party proceeds to visit the White Horse Rapids and Miles
Canyon.

They are both very dangerous looking bits of the river, and
must appear particularly unpleasant to the shivering boatmen
who are forced to navigate their scows through these waters on
the way to Dawson. We are all unanimous in urging the Private
Secretary to hire a scow and attempt the passage of the Rapids,
so that we may have an opportunity of judging whether the
feat is as difficult as it has been described; he is, however,
adamant upon this subject, and declines politely but firmly to
be, as he classically terms it, "butchered to make a public holiday."

Soon after this we proceed by train, on the White Pass and Yukon Railway, to Skagway, being met en route, at the Summit, by a guard of honour of the United States 24th Regiment, and, by tea-time, having bidden farewell to Superintendent Primrose and our escort of North West Mounted Police, we are once more on board the Dominion Government Steamer *Quadra*, which is waiting in the harbour for us, glad indeed to be back in safety in our peaceful quarters on the comfortable government boat.

Within an hour of our embarkation we have weighed anchor and are steaming southwards at full speed, with a favourable breeze astern, commencing the final portion of our return journey to Victoria.

The weather is distinctly colder than it was on our original visit to these parts, there is a severe touch of frost in the even-

ing air, the mountain tops are powdered with a fresh sprinkling of snow and the fireweed on the hillsides has lost its pink
blossom, and, with stalk and leaves tinged to a deep crimson by
the approach of autumn, brightens the countryside with
heather-coloured patches of rich purple.

The Private Secretary has not been feeling well for some
days; he has pains in his head, cold feet and a boiled tongue, all
of which he regards with rising melancholy as the primary
symptoms of impending dissolution. What ails him he cannot
tell, but he is quite certain he has never felt like this before.
The Comptroller cheerfully suggests smallpox, or scurvy, the
latter, he says, from eating too many vegetables, but this choice
of diseases does not commend itself to anyone, and fails in
particular to satisfy the Private Secretary.

On reaching Metlah Catlah, on Sunday, August 26th we go ashore and attend the church, where a service is being held, in the Indian tongue, by the Bishop of Caledonia.[1]

His Lordship is a grand old man, with a long flowing beard, an immaculate tall hat and the regulation gaiters of the stage Bishop. The Comptroller is so impressed that he can with difficulty restrain himself, on landing, from greeting him with "Hail, Caledonia, stern and wild!", a form of address which he considers peculiarly fitting for such an occasion.

The service is brief and choral and the Tsimpsean dialect, in which it is conducted, is melodious and not unpleasing to the

---

[1] "He has been run rather hard by the Salvation Army, and has had to start a band on his own account—" (Lord Minto's Diary, National Library of Scotland).

ear. It is, however, curious to consider that the little village of
Metlah Catlah, which boasts a population of two hundred persons, one half of whom are children, should require the services of a real live Bishop, a rector and seven lady missionaries
(the Comptroller's "Gadarene Virgins"), while many a parish
of ten thousand souls in the East or South of London has to be
content with the ministrations of a single underpaid and over-
worked curate.

In the whole of Metlah Catlah there only exists one unmarried woman, not counting, of course, the seven virgins, and she
only remains a spinster because no other Indian can be found
of sufficiently lofty rank to be her mate.

After service we partake of an excellent luncheon at the
Episcopal Palace, and presently return on board the *Quadra*
and resume our southward voyage.

At about noon on August 28th we arrive at Alert Bay, where,
after luncheon, we land and spend the remainder of the day.

The Private Secretary is gradually recovering his pristine
health and spirits, and, at an early hour, may be seen walking
rapidly up and down the deck, for the purpose of, as he puts it,
"taking the air." By breakfast time he has apparently succeeded
in absorbing most of the atmosphere, as the sea is motionless
and calm, and there is not a breath of wind to ruffle the surface
of the placid waters.

In the afternoon Mr. Spencer, the proprietor and manager
of the Alert Bay Canning Company, takes us out to the Nimp-
kish River, where his fishermen are netting. We arrive in time
to see a haul of about fifty salmon, averaging thirty-five
pounds and belonging to the "satsum" breed, commonly but
not rightly classed by the public among the tribe of "cohoes."

The fishing season here is a short one, lasting from June to
August, inclusive, but, in that time, the seine nets in use can
generally obtain a haul of between seventy and eighty thousand fish. The lucky Company who possess the fishing rights in
this neighbourhood, a privilege for which they pay a merely
nominal price of $200 per seine net per annum, has cleared a
profit of about $25,000 over the last year's fishing.

The Alert Bay Cannery much resembles the many similar

institutions which line this coast, and the various processes by which the fish are prepared for the taste of a fastidious public are as interesting as they are simple.

The salmon, when captured, is deposited on the floor of a large shed, where a ferocious looking Chinaman of the most sanguinary type spears it with a gaff and lifts it onto a gory platform, where another executioner of the Boxer persuasion is grimly awaiting his arrival.

This "yellow-terror" slices the salmon's head off, removes fins, tail and all other outward excrescences and pushes the now unrecognizable carcase into a trough, where a number of Indian women are ready to clean out the more unsavoury parts and cut away all that is not considered fit for human food.

The remains are then passed on, to be sliced up into small

portions some three inches square, and these are poured on to a long table before which a number of women are standing ready to pack them into tins.

These tins have been made in another department, and, at the bottom of each, a thin layer of rough salt has been carefully sprinkled. They are now filled by hand and the salmon is tightly packed into them with the pressure of many Indian fingers, which linger lovingly but in a singularly unappetising manner over the fishy fragments of pink flesh.

The tins are next passed on to another room, where they are weighed, to ascertain whether they contain the correct amount of salmon, by means of a very simple but ingenious machine which casts aside all tins that are under the proper weight (one pound).

The tins which have successfully passed this test are then cleaned and fitted with lids, in the centre of each of which is a small hole, to permit any gas to escape, and eventually roll down a shallow groove, containing liquid solder, from which they presently reappear, tightly welded, tin to lid.

Next the holes in the lids are filled up, the tins are plunged into boiling water, to make certain that there is no leakage, and, if the result is satisfactory (the sign of successful sealing being the absence of any issue of bubbles from the lids) the tins are boiled for some time in a large tank of water.

Each tin is next pricked by hand, to allow of the further escape of any gas which may have been formed internally by the boiling process, resoldered, to render it airtight, and finally placed in a huge iron steam retort, where a pressure of about twenty-five pounds to the square inch is given and a temperature of some three hundred degrees is attained.

The Private Secretary says that he would rather like a Turkish bath at such a temperature and the Aide-de-Camp kindly offers to push him into this infernal machine. He however declines the offer and the Comptroller is heard to mutter to himself something about "the retort courteous."

When the tins have been kept for an hour cooking in this heat, they are plunged into a tank containing a chemical mixture which finally removes all external dirt, and are then carried to a further department where they receive a coating of lacquer and a printed label, are packed in square spruce-wood boxes and are then ready for the market.

The usual day's output of the Cannery consists of about six hundred cases, each of which contains forty-eight one pound tins of cooked salmon.

It is while paying a visit to this factory that we have the supreme pleasure of meeting the man who, as was mentioned in the account of our last stay at Alert Bay, distinguished himself by making a hearty meal off a deceased lady of his acquaintance.

It was with the greatest difficulty that the Private Secretary, who has a curious mind, was prevented from asking this gentleman several searching questions as to the subsequent effects of a diet of human flesh upon the digestion. The Private Secretary is growing fatter every day, and, as he feels intuitively that his personal appearance cannot fail to prove inviting to the critical eye of a cannibalistic connoisseur, he implores us not to leave him alone on shore for any length of time.

Later on in the day we inspect an Indian house, on the outside of which stands a huge and skilfully carved totem pole, more remarkable for the originality of its workmanship than for any great beauty of design.

The habitation of the noble Red Men is a high barnlike building, about fifty yards long by thirty yards broad, with an absolutely bare interior, roughly divided into four parts, each of which is the residence of an Indian family.

On the floor, in the centre of each square, a fire is burning, and the thick, pungent smoke rises upward to escape, as best it may, through apertures roughly hewn in the wooden roof.

Ancient blankets, moth-eaten rugs and dirty remnants of cast-off clothing, huddled together in the different corners, mark the spot where the Indian, in the primitive costume adopted by Adam before the Fall, seeks his simple couch.

Large iron bath-like dishes, half-full of a greasy compound, the native substitute for butter, flat canoe-shaped platters and broken earthenware dishes, still redolent of the remains of the last meal, lie in confusion on the smoke-blackened floor.

Among the Indians it is not apparently considered etiquette to "wash up" after a meal, and consequently to-day's entree of "seal head a la axle-grease" is served up in a dish which still bears a greasy coating of yesterday's concoction of squashed berries and smoked dogfish. A state of things against which the ordinary white man has a distinct and perhaps unnecessary prejudice.

Outside the house stands a wooden wharf; a flat platform situated at the water's edge, serving as a verandah where the replete Red Man and his placid squaw can sit and sun themselves after satisfactorily disposing of the daily banquet.

Early marriages are evidently fashionable in this society, and we come across a small Indian girl of fifteen, who is nursing, with all the responsible solicitude of a full grown mother, her own little six-months-old baby.

It is enough to mention the fact that Alert Bay boasts the services of two missionaries to be certain that the little community is divided into two sections which are continually at war with one another.

In the eyes of the missionary section, at the west end of the village, the east end represents everything that is base and wicked and immoral; the world, the flesh and the devil being especially personified by the Canning Company and all that therein is. It is, however, hardly necessary to state that the wicked east end provides all the inhabitants with work and wages, and that but for the presence of the Cannery, the settlement of Alert Bay would be unable to obtain either labour or the more essential temporal food necessary for its existence.

In the religious west end of the village—and here again one may, perhaps with reason, wonder at the necessity for the presence of two missionaries to watch over a population of only one hundred and thirty souls—the good people look, with all the horror of a holy minority, at the workers in the Cannery, whom they deem guilty of Unbelief, and at the other Indians of the east end, whom they accuse of being unclean, immoral, and, still worse, diseased. Truly a case of "Faith Versus Works."

To-day we also have the opportunity of seeing the Indian school situated at the moral end of the settlement. An excellent institution, no doubt, but conducted, or so at least it appears to the comparative stranger, somewhat after the manner of Mr. Squeers' notorious Academy, "Dotheboys Hall."

"How do you spell 'garden'?" asks the worthy teacher. "That's right," he adds when the boys have given the correct answer, "now go and dig in it for an hour or two!" *Question*: "What is an axe?" *Answer*: "An implement used for chopping wood." "Then go and chop wood till I tell you to stop!" A system of practical education which is extremely good for the physique of the boys and which has the further advantage of allowing the schoolmaster to dispense with the use of household servants, gardener or handy-man.

The walls of the class rooms, as is the case in many similar schools, are decorated with strangely unpleasant prints, representing various of the most painful incidents described in the pages of Holy Writ, and hardly calculated to cheer the heart or stimulate the brain of the average "soaring human boy." Lurid pictures of "The Martyrdom of St. Stephen" or "The Massacre of the Innocents" cannot be beneficial to infantile spirits nor particularly inspiring to the youthful imagination; it is almost criminal to introduce such eye-sores to the notice of the young, when it is remembered that these are probably the sole instances and types of pictorial art which it is the unfortunate scholar's fate to take as his model.

On the blackboard, in the centre of one of the rooms, the following inane sentence has been written in letters of chalk; presumably by the schoolmistress.

"I see a hen, a pen and an egg."

A statement which must necessarily try to the very utmost, the power of credulity of the ordinary sane healthy-minded child, who knows perfectly well that such a collection of objects is very rarely met with in combination. A hen and an egg may very often be observed simultaneously, but it is hard to understand the presence of a pen in a chicken loft, or farm yard; but stay, the article referred to may be a cattle-pen, in which case all is forgiven.

"The cat sees the hen," is another remark, inscribed upon the slate; "Run, hen, run!" A piece of dilatory advice which cannot fail to appear to the average mind to be a trifle superfluous, provided that the hen has been equally quick in observing the cat.

Before leaving Alert Bay we are all induced to buy various

Indian curiosities made by the natives of the place. The Private
Secretary purchases a hideous mask, with which he intends, on
his return home, to keep his children in order, and which will
probably result in giving them a series of fits. The Aide-de-
Camp buys a rattle, used by the local medicine-man to scare
away disease.

When a person is sick the native doctor shakes this rattle
wildly over the invalid's head and gives vent to a series of
frightful yells, intended to induce the evil spirit, who is the
cause of the illness, to retire in alarm. In the case of fever or
neuralgia the cure must be almost more painful than the disease, but the Comptroller affirms that such drastic treatment
frequently saves life, by attracting the patient's attention away
from the subject of death.

We arrive the next afternoon at Comox, a pretty little village
surrounded by tall dark woods and an atmosphere redolent of
English rural life.

Her Majesty's Ship *Warspite* is lying at anchor in the harbour
and we can hear the sailors firing their annual course of mus-
ketry at the butts in the vicinity.

It is here that a certain distinguished Naval Officer, chancing
to show his sword to the Comptroller, casually remarks that he
has been offered as much as $100 for the weapon by an old
Indian chief. "Oh!" says the Comptroller, "I wonder you don't
let him have it, and buy another for $5!" A remark that surely
deserves a place in the very front rank of verbal infelicities,
reflecting, as it does, both upon the character of the officer and
the intrinsic value of his much prized sword.

Our next stop is Nanaimo, a small town on Vancouver
Island, which we reach on August 30th, and where Their Excellencies receive the customary reception and address, take
the usual drive round the town and visit the inevitable hospital.

Nanaimo possesses, according to official statements, a population of about four thousand persons, one thousand of whom
are children, a percentage which strikingly demonstrates the
fertility of the climate and does infinite credit to the painstaking character of the inhabitants.

This little city is also the centre of a district given over to the
interests of coal mining, an industry for which the New Van-

couver Coal Mining Company are largely responsible. To this Company also belongs the admirably managed model farm which is one of the sights of Nanaimo and is laid out, on reclaimed forest land, with praiseworthy enterprise and the most successful results.

The Mayor of the town somewhat surprises His Excellency by commencing the civic address with "Your Majesty," a title hitherto unbestowed upon a Governor General.

As evening draws on the weather grows warmer and the absence of air is almost oppressive, giving the Private Secretary an opportunity of remarking, as we embark once more on our southward journey, that, "the closer we get to Victoria, the closer it gets."

On August 31st, we reach Victoria, where we bid farewell to our worthy Captain, who has watched over our interests and comfort for so long a period.

His friends, and he has many, call him a careful man; his enemies, and he has a few, term him a timid one; his invariable caution has earned for the *Quadra* the nickname of "the daylight boat," owing to the extreme aversion to running after dark which the vessel displays; and, by the maternal anxiety and care shown in his methods of navigating the vessel under his command, he would appear to be as cautious of real as of imaginary dangers.

As we leave the *Quadra* it is very pleasant to consider that the voyage has been uninterrupted by catastrophe, undarkened by accident; that no single day of the many spent on board has been spoilt by bad weather or rough sea; that the officers and crew have been invariably civil, obliging, efficient and satisfactory, and have done all within their power to conduce to our comfort and convenience; and that everything seems to have combined to render the trip a successful one and to ensure that the name of the *Quadra* shall be to us one which is always fraught with the happiest memories.

Chapter 2

September 1st to September 16th

Victoria to MacLeod. Victoria. The Lieutenant Governor. "Labour
Day." Vancouver. New Westminster. Glacier House. The ascent of Mount
Avalanche. Revelstoke. Arrowhead. On the Kootenay Lakes. The Canadian
Pacific Railway Smelting Works at Trail. Rossland. Its mines and public
speakers. Nelson. The Crow's Nest Pass. Cranbrook. Fernie. Michel. Pincher
Creek. Lethbridge. Stirling and Magrath. Lunch with the Mormons. Irriga-
tion. The Blood Reserve of MacLeod.

On September 1st Their Excellencies are publicly welcomed to
Victoria. Addresses are presented at the Drill Hall, where a
large orchestra and a chorus of picked vocalists give renderings
(simultaneously) of "The Maple Leaf" and "The Red, White
and Blue"; and a large lady, with a still small voice, sings "The
Flowers of the Forest" with great feeling; in fact the Comptroller says that she seems to be *feeling* for the right notes all the
time, an accusation which is as unjust as it is libellous.

After this ceremony is over the party, now brilliantly augmented by Their Excellencies' children, who have been living
at Victoria during our visit to Dawson, is driven round the
town to see the illuminations. The evening is finally brought to
a close by a display of fireworks of local manufacture. The
pyrotechnic artist is a Mr. Hitt, and the show is successful
enough to warrant the Private Secretary committing an atro-
cious and elaborately premeditated pun. "Tonight," says this
incorrigible old freak, "Mr. Hitt has made his name!"

The inhabitants of Victoria, and one may almost say the same of the whole population of British Columbia, suffer from an overpowering lethargy and supineness from which nothing will stir them to action. The relaxing climate, the glorious Italian sunshine in which they bask during the summer months and the perpetual downpour of rain in the winter, seem to affect the character and constitution of the residents and endow them with a paralyzing inertia and a general disinclination to work of any kind, both of which are greatly to be deplored.

They greet life with a smiling peace in their eyes, an expression of self-sufficiency in which there is no element of energy, enterprise, or "go."

A pleasanter people it would be hard to find, or a more unbusinesslike.

It is always a matter of considerable curiosity to the stranger in Victoria to discover the manner in which the proprietors of stores and the shopkeepers of that city make a living, since they always appear to be so thoroughly averse to selling any of their goods. To be let alone seems to be their one desire in life, and they look upon the advent of a customer as a disturbing element in an otherwise restful existence, an element which they would pleasurably and readily forgo.

On entering a Victorian shop, for the purpose of making a purchase, you are invariably kept waiting for ten minutes or so before the somnolent gentleman who presides at the counter has wakened up sufficiently to concentrate his attention on the object of your visit.

After apologizing for spoiling his slumbers you probably enquire whether he has got the article you desire. To which he will at once reply that he really doesn't know, he fancies that he hasn't got it, but isn't quite sure. This answer seeming to him to be satisfactory and final, he prepares to return to his former dormant position, and it requires all your entreaties to persuade him to bestir himself sufficiently to go and search for the required article.

When this is found, and the discovery usually takes about half-an-hour, he brings it to you with a grieved air, as of one deeply insulted at being given so much trouble. You then, naturally, ask the price, and he, equally naturally, hasn't the least idea. Like the London cabman, he probably "leaves it to you," or suggests a vague fancy price of his own; or else, if he is unusually energetic, retires into the inner store and wakes up another man (the sleeping partner, says the Private Secretary) to ask.

By the time you have completed your purchase you are reduced to a grovelling state of servile apology for all the inconvenience you have caused by insisting upon buying goods from a man who is so obviously disinclined to sell them.

The Comptroller went into a shop at about half-past five one afternoon to buy fishing tackle. By six o'clock he had purchased about $10 worth and was still up to his eyes in hooks and gut, fumbling his way through a variety of fly-hooks. The shopkeeper thereupon announced to him that, as this was his usual closing hour, he couldn't possibly sell him anything more. It was only with the greatest difficulty that the Comptroller induced the man to keep his store open for another fifteen minutes, as a personal favour, to allow him to spend a further $5.

After this it is hardly necessary to explain that the Americans, across the water, are rapidly taking all the British Columbia trade; are already masters of the shipping; have bought up and are working all of the most valuable industries of the Province, and, by their enterprise, hard work and "push," are earning the cordial dislike of their Canadian cousins who cannot rouse themselves sufficiently to take part in the issues of so active a competition.

The difference in the characteristics of the two countries can be seen most clearly by considering the contrast of the adjacent townships of Seattle and Victoria. At the former the stores are kept open night and day, at the latter the excuse of a football match is sufficient to close every shop in the town.

The one thing that Victoria may be justly proud of is the number of its gardens and the beautiful way in which they are kept and looked after. Gardening would appear to be the only soul-absorbing industry of the town; watering the lawn the most popular pastime; sitting in front of the house, watching the grass grow, the leading occupation of the residents.

There is only one topic of conversation which will rouse a Victorian out of his dormant condition, making his eyes flash with unusual fire and his voice thrill with honest emotion. This is the ever enthralling question of Precedence, with a capital P.

During the few wakeful hours of the day, when the lawn has been adequately watered, and exhausted nature demands a rest, the early Victorian's thoughts are concentrated almost entirely on the question of his social position.

It is curious but worldwide fact that the less recognized rank a man possesses the more he ponders over it and discusses it in the bosom of his family; the more strenuously he clings to his fancied rights, the more earnestly he studies the subject of Precedence.

Send a peer of the realm into dinner after a Member of Parliament, and, in all probability, if your chef is an artist, your soup sufficiently hot, your Perrier Jouet properly cold, your Lafite of the same temperature as the room, and your wife a good-looking woman, he will dine with you again. Allow the wife of a retired Indian Major to walk into the dining-room in front of the better half of a provincial mayor (and mayors are singularly unlucky in their matrimonial selections) and your future chances of entertaining a civic functionary at your hospital board are practically nil.

If, by a regrettable mistake, the niece of a chimney sweep were to be given precedence over the daughter of a proprietor of the leading local dry-goods emporium, the consequences would be more appalling than the mind can imagine. The heavens would probably fall and the earth cease to revolve upon its axis; the injured damsel would go into a trance, while her indignant parent had a stroke in the drawing-room. It is also quite possible that the latter would continue to have strokes until the error was rectified.

With reference to Victoria, however, this criticism is not aimed at the few recognized leaders of society whose position is unquestionably accredited and who are naturally above such petty distinctions.

British Columbia possesses probably the most charming and courteous Lieutenant Governor of any Province in the Dominion, and she does well to be proud of her possession. A Seigneur of the old school, amiable to a fault, with an unrivalled charm of manner and courtly old-world grace which wins all hearts, Sir Henri Joly possesses in a marked degree that "joie de vivre," that enthusiasm of existence which conduces to happiness, and, by his unfailing endeavours to make others happy, he has won for himself a golden measure of that happiness which he so thoroughly deserves. His Honour is still as young as he was some thirty years ago, and, by the example of his marvellous energy and zeal, may yet hope to rouse from its overwhelming lethargy the population whose good fortune it is to be ruled by so popular a Governor.

It was while shopping in Victoria that Her Excellency was the victim of the first and only piece of deliberate discourtesy met with in Western Canada.

The memory of so delightful a city, where all classes proved themselves as polite as they were hospitable is only marred by this one instance of studied incivility, an incident which occurred at the store of a frame-maker named Somers, in Government Street, where a conceited and ill-mannered assistant considered that to be disobliging to the first lady in the land was a sign of independence.

There is in every country a certain type of individual who imagines that rudeness is a sign of independent will; who considers that a free citizen is free to be as discourteous to his social superior as he wishes, and who cannot differentiate between the liberty he enjoys as a birthright and the liberties he takes from illbreeding.

And, perhaps, in Canada, where freedom is valued so highly, the class of independent young men, revelling in the arrogance of their own self-sufficiency, is more offensive than elsewhere.

We have seen two students of McGill University, Montreal, both young enough to know better, remain seated and with covered heads in a room through which Their Excellencies passed. Had any other lady entered the room they would no doubt have risen and removed their hats, but, because the visitor happened to be Lady Minto, they feared that an act of ordinary politeness would appear servile and snobbish, and preferred an attitude of deliberate incivility, mistaken by them for a sign of independence, whereas in reality the feelings which prompted it are of the very essence of snobbishness.

In Ottawa, the Capital of our Dominion, the great majority

of people, all, in fact, except the very upper class, will, if possible, ignore the presence of the Governor General or his wife in the street, fearful that, by raising their hat or showing any common courtesy to the representative of Her Majesty the Queen, they may risk the loss of the freedom which they misunderstand as highly as they prize.

In Quebec politeness is a more common commodity, inherited no doubt from French ancestry; in Toronto and the West, where the English element is very strong, it may also be met with, but elsewhere the outward civility of the man in the street is only conspicuous by its absence.

September 3rd is "Labour Day," so called because it is a public holiday, upon which nobody does any work and the tradesman goes to sleep at home instead of behind the counter of his shop.

Today, as on the occasion of an English Bank Holiday, it is the custom of the inhabitants to seek recreation and enjoyment on the seashore or in the woods, whither they take their meals and where they spend the day, seated on the hard ground in the acutest physical discomfort.

The popular idea of enjoyment all over the English-speaking portion of the globe appears to be the same. Two men, five women and about fourteen children hire a large boat, capable of holding six persons with comfort, into which they all contrive to scramble, and put out to sea. Each of the children and the two most energetic women taken an oar and flap the water convulsively but with little progressive result, while the remainder of the party change hats with one another and lounge at the bottom of the boat, where they sing "Soldiers of the Queen" at the top of their voice, amid a chaotic surrounding of empty bottles and sticky oranges.

In accordance with the general wish of the party we take a steam launch in the afternoon and go up "The Gorge," an arm of the sea between Esquimalt and Victoria, to a suitable grassy bank, where we can land and have tea. The sunshine is brilliant and we lie in uncomfortable attitudes on the mossy ground, watching the kettle refuse to boil and sharing jam-sandwiches with the numerous large spiders which abound in these woods.

The children naturally insist upon lighting a fire, the smoke from which makes further food impossible. The spiders who object to smoking on principle, together with those of their human sympathizers who object to being smoked, hurry away to a safe distance, leaving the scene of the fire to the younger children, who revel in the choking fumes, and to a few of the hardier spiders who apparently inhale the smoke from their burning dwellings with perfect enjoyment.

On the next day Their Excellencies visit the High Schools and are much struck by the appearance of the children. So many of these are strikingly pretty, with glorious complexions and masses of lovely hair, which contrast strongly with the sallow skins and scantier locks of the majority of the school children in Eastern Canada. Health and happiness seem to be imprinted on the faces of these merry young persons, and it is a positive pleasure to spend a morning basking in the sunshine of their smiles.

On September 4th a Fulldress Reception is held at the Legislative Assembly, where about two hundred persons make their bow.

The function is a distinct success, although the number of attendances is comparatively small. This can be accounted for by the fact that many of the inhabitants are unable to summon up sufficient energy to make up their minds as to whether they shall go or not, and the time flies by before they have come to any final decision.

On September 5th we cross over to Vancouver, where Their Excellencies are received by the Mayor and civic functionaries, visit three hospitals, and, in the evening, attend a ball given in their honour at the Vancouver Hotel.

The Vice-Regal party is now brilliantly augmented by the addition of the Ladies Eileen and Ruby Elliot, who are to accompany us for the remainder of the journey home. The smaller children are left behind at Victoria and will not be seen again until we reach Ottawa in October.

At Vancouver we are also shown over a large saw-mill where we can but wonder at the extraordinary manner in which the huge trees, some of them from fifteen to twenty feet in diameter, are handled, preparatory to being cut up for trade purposes. Great merciless arms of machinery seize this gigantic lumber and roll it about as conveniently and relentlessly as

134 though it were mere firewood, while the powerful saws cut
their way through masses of the stoutest timber with the ease of
a knife slicing butter.

The next morning we proceed by steamer, up the Fraser
River, to New Westminster, where the customary reception
takes place and the ceremony of planting a maple tree in the
public park, an act gracefully performed by Her Excellency, is
added to the usual list of addresses and functions.

New Westminster was the original capital of British Columbia, before Vancouver Island was incorporated into the province. The whole city was burnt to the ground only two years
ago, in September, 1898, and it says much for the zeal of the
residents that at the present moment the houses are rising on
all sides from their ruins with remarkable celerity, and that the
inhabitants already exceed in number the population of the
city previous to the occurrence of the disastrous conflagration.

Of the few large buildings untouched by the flames the two
which stand prominently out are the penitentiary and the
lunatic asylum. The latter is generally crowded with inmates,
and may well be so, considering that the percentage of insane
persons in British Columbia, .70 per 1000 of the inhabitants, is
far in excess of that of any other country in the world. This fact
is attributed, by the residents, to the custom prevalent among
the families of England of sending the weaker-minded of their
relations to Western Canada to earn their living on farms or
ranches, and thus ridding the mother country of a number of
probable candidates for Hanwell or Broadmoor; an explana-
tion which cannot be regarded as altogether satisfactory.

At New Westminster we visit the Cold Storage, which is one
of the sights of the town; where thousands of salmon from the
Fraser River are chemically frozen and packed for the foreign
markets. It is an odd sensation, in the middle of summer, to
find oneself in a room whose temperature is below zero, where
the workmen are clad in furs, and to see the huge fish standing
like solid marble statues all round the walls. Whether the experience is a healthful one or likely to be a protection against
chills is another matter.

On the same afternoon we bid farewell to New Westminster
and proceed, by special train, to Glacier House, where it is our

intention to spend a restful Friday to Sunday, for the purpose of recovering from the effects of a combination of perpetual travelling, endless functions and the "hootch" of Dawson City, which latter clings for a long time to the system with the worst results.

The Canadian Pacific Railway Hotel at Glacier House is the most comfortable we have yet visited. The food is so excellent that the Private Secretary considers it a positive sin to stop eating, and the whole arrangements of the hotel are clean and comfortable in the extreme.

During our stay here His Excellency and the Comptroller spend the whole of one day climbing Mount Avalanche, a feat which requires some five hours in the accomplishment and from which they return, after a further descent of three hours, worn out but triumphant, and bursting with the desire to impart to all a narration of their thrilling experiences.

Meanwhile the remainder of the party, with simpler tastes, make the ascent of the mountain at the back of the Hotel, and finally reach Lake Marrion where a magnificent view of the "loop" of the Selkirks can be obtained.

The ascent takes about an hour and a quarter and is facilitated by the services of a pony hired for the occasion. This unfortunate animal, which is about the size of an ordinary dog, carries Eileen up the steepest gradient without a murmur, while Her Excellency and Ruby hold on to its tail and are towed up in rear; a mode of progression which reminds Her Excellency that she has promised to become the patroness of a society for the prevention of cruelty to animals in Victoria.

Glacier House is not a suitable place in which to spend the winter, as it has often been known to snow here for three weeks without cessation, and the actual snowfall for the last year was forty-two and half feet; but one can imagine no pleasanter place for a short visit during the summer season.

The hotel is provided with some half dozen Swiss guides, polite and courteous men, who remain here from May till the middle of September, and who will convey guests of the Hotel up the adjacent mountains with great care and for a small fee.

His Excellency and the Comptroller, who are neither of them in the best of condition, certainly did not bargain for so stiff a climb as that afforded them by the ascent of Mount Avalanche, and, on eventually reaching the summit, where other previous climbers had left souvenirs of their exploits, they deposit, as a memento of the day's toil, a bottle containing a piece of paper with the following inscription:

Notice, To all whom it may concern.

This is to certify that at noon on the seventh day of September, in the year of Our Lord 1900, the Governor General of Canada, accompanied by his Comptroller of the Household, accomplished the ascent of Mount Avalanche, and proudly placed a statement to that effect on this hallowed spot. After the harrowing experiences of the ascent the question of a safe return to the bosoms of their respective families appears to them an entirely problematical one.

P.S. 12:30 P.M. After assimilating the entire ration of whiskey with which they have provided themselves, together with the whole of the brandy belonging to the guides, the mountaineers are prepared to undertake the perilous descent. Friends will please accept this, the only intimation. English and Provincial papers please copy.

During this ascent they are much struck by the number of marmots which surround their path. Whole families of these engaging little animals, mother marmots, father marmots and baby marmots (or, as the Comptroller prefers to term them, "marmots, parmots and marmosets") flock around them, and, at a whistle from the guide, come out of their holes to gaze inquisitively at the explorers. The whole spare time of these little rodents is employed in collecting food for the winter months, during which they remain buried under the deep snow.

The Private Secretary had originally intended to accompany the Avalanche party, but backed out of it at the last moment. He believes in what he calls the "three E's," Energy, Exercise, and Eno, as a sure preventive of sickness or melancholia; but, at the same time, considers it a duty to his constitution to avoid over-exertion in any form. He is a great stickler for duty is the Private Secretary.

His costume for mountaineering is conspicuous for the immaculate coal black satin tie with which it is crowned, and he explains that this thoughtful little touch of sable has been

added in deference to the fact of the Court being, at present, in
mourning.

It is pointed out to him that such precision in the etiquette of dress is hardly necessary at an altitude of more than five thousand feet above the level of the sea, but he is firm upon the subject. "If," he says, "I was all alone on a desert island during a period of public mourning, and had no clothes at all except cockleshells, I should consider it my bounden duty to put a dark band of seaweed round my left arm and make for myself a black tie out of the bark of a mahogany tree." A noble sentiment surely!

At Glacier House we have an opportunity of making a further acquaintance with Mr. Duchesnay, the Superintendent of this section of the Canadian Pacific Railway. A French Canadian of unfailing courtesy, an explorer of varied experience, and altogether a most interesting man. With one single exception the Superintendents all along the line have been excessively obliging and polite, but Mr. Duchesnay stands out pre-eminent in our memory by reason of his unfailing willingness to give assistance, and his excessive anxiety to make our journey, at least upon his own section, a pleasant and agreeable one; a task in which he amply succeeds.

We leave Glacier on September 9th for Arrowhead, spending half an hour at Revelstoke on the way.

Revelstoke is one of the many mushroom mining settlements of Western Canada, which are rapidly developing into small and flourishing towns. One is much struck here by the number of little model habitations, built apparently on the pattern of the doll's house of one's infancy, which possessed a square green front door, four square green windows, of identical shape and size, and a red chimney situated in the exact centre of the conical roof.

With his thoughts reverting to those distant but happy days of his early childhood the Private Secretary says that he is constantly expecting the whole front of any one of these Revelstoke dwellings to swing open on its hinges, disclosing two rooms, of similar proportions, extending across a whole length of the house, and situated, exactly one over the other. The upper one, if the Private Secretary's recollection of a doll's house is correct, would usually be a sleeping apartment, in which a huge double-bed, an old-fashioned four-poster with curtains, extends over almost the entire floor, while a tiny tin wash-hand-stand leans meekly up in one of the corners. The floor below, to which by-the-bye, probably owing to temporary absentmindedness on the part of the architect, there is no means of descent from above, save by climbing from one window to another, generally consists of a drawingroom, simply but artistically furnished with four wedgewood chairs, set at precise intervals all round the wall, as if for family prayers; while a slender round table, in the centre of the room, supports a large pot, containing an artificial plant whose topmost flowers almost scrape the ceiling. A gold looking-glass, which occupies the greater part of one wall, completes the picture.

Occasionally the lower room is a kitchen; this fact being conveyed by the presence of a black range and a large four-legged wooden table, upon which are glued plates containing crimson lobsters, slices of underdone beef of an unhealthy colouring and bunches of unripe grapes and faded lemons.

At Arrowhead we board the s.s. *Kootenay*, a sternwheeler owned by the Canadian Pacific Railway, whose steamboat services run daily, to and from Robson, all the year round.

In this boat we start early the next morning, passing through the upper and lower Arrow Lakes and down the Columbia River, in the most perfect weather and surrounded by the glorious scenery for which the Kootenay district is so justly famous.

The river is edged with natural lawns of short green sward, forming a picturesque foreground to the high red-brown hills which rise in rear, and providing a good field of pasture for the many cattle which graze along the water-side.

Towards noon we pass the uninhabited village of Brooklyn, a settlement founded by the workmen employed in the construction of the Rossland, Grand Forks and Greenwood Railway, and deserted on the completion of the line. This railroad was built at the enormous cost of $60,000 per mile, and, as it is hardly necessary to say, is in the hands of that great Canadian octopus, the Canadian Pacific Railway Co.

Arrived at Robson, we take the train once more, and proceed

South to Trail, where we are shown the immense smelting works which have here been erected by the Railway Company.

Whereas the precious metals can be obtained from the ore of the placer mines in the Klondyke by the process of washing; and in the quartz mines, such as the one we visited at the Lake of the Woods, or the famous Treadwell Mine of Alaska, by the stamping and crushing process, known as "free-milling"; it is only by "smelting" that the refractory ore in most of the mines of the Kootenay district can be induced to give up the treasure it contains.

Nearly all the surrounding mines send their ore to Trail, where it is dumped into the depositories ready for its reception. Samples of the ore from the various claims are then crushed and assayed, and, from the result of this assay, the value of the ore is determined. The Smelting Company then buys the ore from the original proprietors, and thus accepts all risks, prior to the various processes necessary for obtaining the different metals.

The ore is, first of all, roasted in large blast furnaces, for the purpose of getting rid of as much as possible of the sulphur naturally contained. The result is then smelted to an intense heat and poured off, in a liquid state, into iron tanks. All the worthless deposit, known as "slag," floats on the surface of these vats, and is removed; the valuable remainder, technically termed "amalgam," is allowed to cool, until it hardens into a compact mass, when it is broken up, packed in sacks and sent to New York or elsewhere, to await further refinement and the separation of the gold, silver, copper or lead contained. It is calculated that about one thousand tons of ore can be smelted daily at the Canadian Pacific Railway Works here, but this amount is seldom attempted or attained.

Soon after leaving Trail the railroad becomes excessively steep, the grade being occasionally as much as four percent, and the line curves in a continuously serpentine manner; so that although the City of Rossland comes into view at about six P.M., when it appears to be only a few miles away and passengers instinctively reach for their hats and bags, it is not until nearly an hour later that the train arrives by a circuitous route, the level rising some 2,300 feet in eleven miles at the long-looked-for terminus.

Rossland is a mining city of about six thousand inhabitants; the numerous wooden houses of the settlement are scattered over the slopes of adjoining hills, and, at night, when the town is lighted up, give a very picturesque effect to the scene.

Here Their Excellencies receive the customary address, the town is illuminated in their honour, a beacon flares out from the highest mountain in the vicinity, but lately christened "Mount Roberts" in memory of the South African war, and the evening closes with a Public Reception.

The next morning we pay a visit to two of the largest mines in the district, the "Centre Star," which is about six hundred feet deep, and the "War Eagle," whose pitmouth is situated high up on the slope of the Red Mountain, whence a magnificent view of Rossland and the surrounding country can be obtained, and whose shaft descends one thousand feet into the earth.

Before going down a mine it is necessary, for the proper protection of his ordinary clothes, for the self-respecting citizen to assume an attire which closely resembles that usually adopted by the inmates of a penitentiary. While donning his convict garb the Private Secretary can hardly restrain his emotion, as a host of memories, recalled by such a costume, come crowding into what he is pleased to call his mind. Her Excellency and the girls look particularly well in this criminal attire and it only requires the addition of a couple of candles, one to be held in each hand, to complete a picture which is as attractive as it is unique.

After a large luncheon, at the office of the British American Corporation, the party is driven to the famous Le Roi mine, which is probably, taking into consideration the amount of present development, one of the largest and most promising mines on this continent. To the inexperienced eye of the ignorant it appears as if the output of ore were inexhaustible; some of the seams being, in places, as much as one hundred and fifteen feet wide, while the main shaft reaches a depth of nine hundred feet.

In the engine rooms of the Le Roi Company a sufficiency of compressed air can be generated to produce a twelve hundred and fifty horse power, by means of which one hundred and twenty-five or more drills can be used.

The mine is entirely worked by means of these drills, which are employed to bore holes in the ore seams, into which charges of dynamite can be placed for blasting purposes; the material thus loosened being then conveyed to the surface in large iron buckets or "skips."

It is in one of these "skips" that we are let down into the mine for a depth of seven hundred feet, where we are surprised to find the air as clear and pure as on the surface and where the absence of dampness, so prevalent and unpleasant a feature of most mines, is quite remarkable.

Our "skip" is of a new pattern, capable of containing five tons, and consequently supplies sufficient ground space for the accommodation of the Comptroller's feet, and our descent is fortunately a slow one; but we have an opportunity of watching other skips making the journey, at a pace which is swift enough to take the strongest breath away or make the sternest digestion pale.

Some of the old-fashioned skips, still in use here, and with a carrying capacity of two tons, can be filled with ore, raised to the surface from a depth of five hundred feet, and emptied at the rate of four hundred and thirty-nine in four hundred and twenty minutes; a speed which would not allow any unfortunate human occupant of this means of conveyance much opportunity for quiet earnest thought.

Unlike the other mines at Rossland, which send their ore to Trail to be smelted, the Le Roi has its own smelting works at Northport, a town situated about twelve miles distant, in United States territory.

The claim on which this rich mine is now worked was originally sold, by the proprietors, to the local Recorder at Nelson, a certain Colonel Topping, for $7.50, that being the amount of the sum required for the payment of recording fees on three claims discovered by these men. They were themselves unable to produce sufficient money to pay these fees, and consequently, offered one of the claims to the Recorder, on consideration that he would supply the required cash for the three claims. This lucky claim was subsequently bought from him for a few thousand dollars, and the Le Roi Mine could now be sold for almost any sum up to forty millions.

This evening His Excellency and his staff are entertained at a civic banquet, where feeding and speechmaking are continued until two A.M. Judging by the amount of superfluous and unnecessary oratory exhibited on this occasion one would imagine Rossland to be the home of many would-be rhetoricians, who but seldom have an opportunity of exercising their barnstorming powers.

One after another they rise to their feet, and, in speeches of some hours in duration, alternately soar to the giddiest heights of elocution and sink exhausted to the lowest depths of fatuous bathos, in a self-assertive manner and with a studied frequency which makes their utterances almost insupportable.

There is an absolute lack of bashfulness about the orators of Rossland, which renders their speeches less notable for any power of thought or gift of expression than for the utterly satisfied way in which they give vent to amazing feelings of the smuggest and most blatant self-sufficiency.

What other persons would be apt to term boastfulness, they regard as natural pride; and their idea of patriotism is what, to other eyes and ears, must closely resemble the worst form of jingoism, reared upon a monument of the most consummate self-conceit.

To make use of a hackneyed quotation, which nevertheless seems to adequately fit the frame of mind of these gentlemen, they may be accused with perfect truth of "revelling in the exuberance of their own verbosity!"

During his stay at Rossland His Excellency is daily waited upon by a "coloured gentleman," a great character in his way locally known as "Colonel Jackson." This old man is an emancipated slave, and his costume consists of a blue coat with brass buttons, held in at the waist by a tartan sash; bright yellow trousers, ornamented by an inconceivably monstrous pattern of red and brown checks; and white woolen gloves. On the bosom of his coat he wears a number of medals, won at various culinary competitions, he being an adept in the art of cookery, and, in consideration of his service to His Excellency's person, a further medal is cast and presented to him, as a fitting memorial of so auspicious an occasion.

On September 12th we leave Rossland, with feelings of gratitude for our hospitable reception, but with little real regret, and proceed, via Robson, to Nelson, B.C.

On our way we pass the Bonnington Falls, from which the power is obtained to supply Rossland and the surrounding towns with electricity, and reach Nelson at about noon.

Nelson is the oldest settlement of the Kootenay district, and, as such, regards Rossland with much the same feelings as Vancouver expresses towards Victoria.

Its inhabitants are fewer than those of the rival city, more apathetic perhaps, certainly more unassuming and pleasanter to meet. It possesses an electric street-car service, which leads nowhere, and a public park, which at present consists of a desert of loose stones and a couple of wooden benches.

The town is pleasantly situated on the edge of the Kootenay
Lake, where good sailing is to be enjoyed and whence a very
pretty view of the little city can be obtained.

After the usual address, an aimless ride on the tram-car and
a short sail on the lake, a Reception is held in the evening, and
the Vice-Regal party, escorted by the town band and the local
band of the Salvation Army, both playing different tunes at the
same instant, proceeds on board the private train, which is
presently to be launched on scows and towed down the lake to
Kootenay Landing during the night.

The next morning the journey is resumed, from Kootenay
Landing, over the Crow's Nest branch of the Canadian Pacific
Railway, one of the roughest, most jolting and worst ballasted
portions of that otherwise estimable line.

On reaching Cranbrook, at about ten A.M., we learn that
"Diamond Jubilee" has won the St. Leger, a race which takes
place in England this afternoon! And our attention is attracted
by the antics of an intoxicated Irishman on the platform, who,
as an old soldier of Her Majesty's 18th Regiment, is celebrating
the anniversary of Tel-el-kebir in a fittingly exuberant fashion.
He addresses himself vaguely to the train, and his remarks
consist almost entirely of a series of interrogations, to which he
thoughtfully supplies his own answers. "Where," he asks, refer-
ring to the Boer war, "do the Dutch fight?" "Behind rocks!" he
continues, there being no effort on anyone's part to find a
suitable reply to this query. "Where do the English fight!" he
fiercely demands. "Behind the Irish!" A statement which is
received with much general amusement. After this blast of elo-
quence exhausted nature demands a stimulant, and he departs,
in a glow of conscious success, to search for further invigorating
refreshment of a liquid nature at the nearest bar. He is last seen
drinking his own health, with full Highland honours, at a local
saloon, from which he presently emerges "brimming over with
happy laughter" and flushed with a feeling of kindly indulgence
and toleration towards mankind at large.

Our next stop is Fernie, where Her Excellency is met by a
Committee of local ladies and presented with an enamelled
spoon and a few words of welcome, to which she fittingly replies.

At Michel, Major Ferry, the able and delightful Commissioner of the North West Mounted Police and Superintendent Deane, come on board the train, with the intention of escorting us through the North West Territories.

We are now running through the Crow's Nest Pass, where a surfeit of magnificent scenery is displayed to the eye of the traveller, and the train is soon skirting the Old Man's River, which sprouts from a cave situated close to the railroad track, the water having its original source in a lake some two miles higher up in the hills.

After passing Pincher Creek, whose volunteers have earned such a gallant reputation among the Colonial troops fighting for the Empire in South Africa, we find the prairies opening out before us, and, towards evening, arrive at Lethbridge, where we are to be the guests of Mr. Galt, the most prominent and best known man in the district.

Lethbridge, a small coal-mining centre, situated in Alberta (North West Territories), is a singularly uninteresting, unattractive looking village, dotted down in the very middle of a boundless expanse of plain; and possessing no natural scenery, save a display of wonderful sunset effects; no view, save the horizon.

It is consequently with feelings of some irritation that we wake on September 14th to find a snowstorm raging without and a heavy wind sweeping rudely across the prairie.

In spite, however, of the inclemency of the weather, we make an early start, after a still earlier breakfast, and take the train to Stirling, which we reach at about ten A.M.

Stirling is but a very small Mormon settlement, of about four hundred souls, who immigrated here, some thirteen months ago, from the Salt Lake Valley. We arrive in time for a meeting at the village chapel, where a number of the residents are gathered to welcome Their Excellencies.

The personal appearance of these Mormons is very striking, most of the men being of good education and of strong, independent character, and it is a small wonder that, as colonists, they are admittedly so satisfactory and successful.

From Stirling we ride on, accompanied by a police escort, to Magrath, a distance of about seventeen miles, and arrive there in time for luncheon, prepared for us at the house of one of the leading residents.

Magrath is another Mormon settlement, of the same population as Stirling, and it is here our privilege to meet with two of the Presidents of the Mormon Sect, Mr. Cannon and Mr. Smith, who happen to be paying a brief visit to this locality.

The Mormons at present number about four hundred and forty thousand, and are governed by a President, Mr. Snow, and an Advisory Council of two, the gentlemen whose acquaintance it is our pleasure to make to-day.

Next to these three, in the order of precedence, come the "Twelve Apostles," from whose ranks the head of the church is elected by the remainder, as a vacancy occurs, subject to the consent of the people. The newly elected President is allowed to select any two of the "apostles" as his council, and with these three rest all questions of religion, orthodoxy, etc.

Each Mormon settlement possesses a "bishop," who is chosen and appointed for his sound business-like qualifications more than for any other reason, and who differs from the bishops of other churches in that he receives no salary at all and is expected to be able to support himself. His duties are mostly secular; he looks after the interests of his flock, attends to the necessities of the poor, and is, in effect, the headman of the settlement.

All young men of any character or repute among the Mormons are sent out as missionaries, for a few years, during the earlier stages of their manhood, and thus have an opportunity of broadening their minds by travel and of becoming capable men of the world, who return to their early profession with wider views and a vast experience, which must prove of inestimable value to their fellow-residents. The efficiency of this missionary work can be estimated from the fact that the number of converts who emigrate from Europe each year is close upon ten thousand.

The Mormons no longer regard polygamy as legal or desirable, and confine their attentions exclusively to a single wife, or, if they are married prior to the date of this new "Revelation," to the senior of the wives whom they have already wedded; a system which appears to be as hard upon the husband as upon the deserted wives. On this being explained to the Comptroller he at once renounces all ideas of embracing Mormonism, a religion after which he had long had ardent hankerings; with him, he admits, the senior wife idea goes completely against the grain.

In this part of Alberta the Canadian North West Irrigation Company has started a system of fertilising the soil by means of canals and water ways, which is likely to prove of great value to the country at large. Nowhere could they look for or obtain better or more suitable employees than among the Mormons, who were the first of the Anglo-Saxon race to cultivate the science of irrigation, and who have carried the art of fertilizing waste places to the highest possible pitch in Salt Lake City.

Late in the afternoon we leave Magrath and return to Lethbridge, a ride of about twenty-three miles, accomplished, in a gale of wind and rain, in just over two hours, and only enlivened by the sight of a large timber wolf, viewed on the prairie some two hundred yards away from the head of the cavalcade.

Owing to the countless badger holes and the burrows of innumerable gophers and other little denizens of the plains, there is always a certain element of danger involved in a rapid ride across the prairie, but the average horse of the country has learnt caution with experience and seldom puts his foot into the many traps set for him by Nature.

At an early hour on the following morning we take the train to MacLeod and from there ride out some twelve miles from the Town to the Indian Blood Reserve.

The Bloods are a tribe of the great Blackfoot Nation, and, until recently, their chief was Red Crow, a well-known Indian, who died but a short time ago, and for whom the Reserve is still mourning.

As we approach the settlement, the Indian chiefs come riding out to meet Their Excellencies, and, after formal introduction and much handshaking, escort us back into the circle of their camp.

Each Reserve possesses one big chief, to whom the Government allows an annuity of $25 and a scarlet gold-braided coat, and a number of minor chiefs, who are provided with a smaller sum annually and are given blue coats with brass buttons.

Every year, at Treaty time, a sum of $5 is paid for every Indian man, woman or child on the Reserve, and proportional rations are provided bi-weekly in ample quantities.

At the pow-wow, which takes place in the afternoon, we have the honour of an introduction to many chiefs and bucks, whose appellations are as striking as their war-painted and be-blanketed appearance. Thunder Chief, the head man of the Bloods, who is expected to succeed Red Crow at the next election; Crow Chief, who belongs to the Peigan tribe and is here on a visit; and Blackfoot Old Woman, a minor chief, stand prominently out as orators and spokesmen. Among those present we also notice Sweet Grass, Crop-ear Wolf, Taking-the-Sun-Down, Tail-feathers-round-his-neck, Eddy-springing-in-a-crowd, and Old-Man-afraid-of-Horses.

In the course of the pow-wow one of the Indians, of the name of Straggling Wolf, observes the humble chronicler of these lines making a note upon his shirt cuff, whereupon he immediately christens him "Morning Paper." The Comptroller, who remains seated during the proceedings, to the great indignation of a local chief, who is himself anxious to secure a place in the front row, is promptly given the happy name of "Young-man-not-afraid-of-chairs!"

We are also introduced to the local medicine-man and snake-charmer, who, producing from his pocket a fullgrown and dangerous looking rattlesnake, places its head affectionately between his front teeth and allows us to take a photograph of him in this unique position. It appears that he has a particularly warm feeling towards this snake and cannot bear to be parted from it for a moment, as it killed his only child some little time ago!

The one complaint of the Indians is that they do not get enough food, but, when it is remembered that their daily ration consists of one and a quarter pounds of meat and half a pound of flour for every living soul on the reserve, regardless of sex or age, it must be admitted that this grievance of theirs is hardly a reasonable one.

The really needful thing, of which they require a fuller measure, is work, to occupy that long portion of the day during which they sit and ponder idly over their imaginary illtreatment.

Chapter 3

September 17th to October 13th

MacLeod to Ottawa. Okotoks. Calgary. The Sarcee Reserve. A day
with the prairie chicken. Edmonton. St. Albert. "The Minto" Gold Dredge.
Gleichen. The Blackfoot Reserve. Regina. Saskatoon. Prince Albert. Duck
Lake. In Camp at Batoche. Fish Creek. Her Excellency leaves for Winnipeg
via Brandon & returns to Ottawa. The Ride from Batoche via Vermilion
Lake. Humboldt & Touchwood to Qu'Appelle. Poplar Point. Duck shooting
on Lake Manitoba. The return to Ottawa. Home again.

Leaving MacLeod on the evening of September 16th we wake
on the following morning at Okotoks, a little station situated
between MacLeod and Calgary, some thirty miles from the
latter, and are much surprised to find snow lying half an inch
deep on the ground and a cold rain falling in torrents.

We spend a peaceful Sunday at this place, driving over to
luncheon at the Quorn Ranch, the property of Mr. Swann, and
occupying the remainder of the day with arrears of long post-
poned correspondence.

On our drive to the ranch we are much amused by the antics
of the numerous gophers, curious little animals, something
after the species of the chipmunk, who peer inquisitively at us
from all sides of the road as we pass.

The more one sees of the immense numbers of holes and
toe-traps caused by these creatures and by the badgers and
coyotes, the more one wonders at the surefootedness of the
horse of the country, who can be left to make his way with

perfect safety across the most honeycombed portion of the prairie.

Speaking on this subject the Comptroller contends that "gopher" is a very difficult word to which to find a suitable rhyme, and, after many attempts on the part of the "gilded staff," the following is adjudged to be the most successful solution to this difficulty:

A timid young lady of Ophir
Was crossing from Calais to Dopher
  When up came a loafer,
  Sat down on the sofa,
And called her his "dear little gopher"!

The Aide-de-Camp is, needless to say, guilty of this production.

On Monday morning we reach Calgary, the most important place in, but not the capital of, the North West Territories, and, at noon, we mount our horses once more and ride out to the Sarcee Reserve, some nine miles north of the town.

The Sarcee Indians are a branch of the Beaver Tribe; they number, on this reserve, only about a couple of hundred, their present chief, Bull Head, being a very old man with rapidly failing health.

The Sarcee language is so difficult that no white man has ever yet mastered it, and in consequence of this, the Indians are forced to use the Blackfoot tongue in their intercourse with the whites.

Their Excellencies get a most magnificent reception at this Reserve, the Indians turning out in all the glory of their war-paint; chiefs and bucks in feathers and furs, squaws and papooses in beautifully beaded costumes of tastefully blended colouring.

On nearing the settlement we find the inhabitants waiting to welcome us. In two rows they line the trail, seated on their little ponies, some of which are also bedaubed with paint in honour of the occasion, and, as we ride up, they give vent to wild yells, fire their rifles (loaded with ball cartridge) repeatedly into the air, and accompany us at a wild gallop, into the precincts of the camp.

The Indians subsequently give an exhibition of dancing, to the accompaniment of music, at least it is supposed that the sounds produced are intended and imagined to be musical, provided by a band consisting of four sturdy performers on the drum. These misguided men sit round their instrument, which is evidently of home manufacture, and hammer it with sticks, at the same time singing a weird and wonderfully unattractive tune, suggestive of the dischords produced by a beginner on the bag-pipes in his attempts to coax his instrument of torture into making up its mind to start.

Of the terpsichorean performance the "goose dance" appears to be the favorite. In this the bucks and squaws, divided into two parties, according to sex, surround the orchestra, facing inwards, and the whole circle gyrates slowly and painfully round this centre; the point of the dance lying in the fact that only one foot is used, and the result being a motion which

suggests the sideways entrance of the ghost of Fabian, in the Lyceum edition of *The Corsican Brothers*.

In the "war dance" the only step which the chiefs perform is that of hopping twice on each leg alternately, with an occasional additional wriggling of the central part of the body, intended to give a spice to the performance, and recalling, to the Private Secretary, a dance which he once witnessed, either in Paris, at the Quartier Latin, or at Rossland, he can't remember which!

The privilege of being allowed to join the dance is only allowed to a small clique of the Indian nobility and is much valued. Personally, the Aide-de-Camp says, he has no wish to make an ass of himself in this way, though he has no doubt that the temptation to some people (here he looks pointedly at the Private Secretary) must be a strong one. The Private Secretary admits he has never seen anything like it, and doesn't suppose that even the Aide-de-Camp has ever witnessed, outside of Hanwell, a similar performance.

The squaws, when dancing, keep their eyes fixed on the ground and assume an air of most complete modesty, singularly out of keeping with their general character.

The presence of white men always has this effect upon them, and, though absolutely deficient in the very rudiments of morality, or even decency, in their mutual intercourse with one another their sensitiveness before white men is so strong that they will hardly permit a doctor to examine their lungs or apply his stethoscope to them.

In the afternoon the Indians are induced, by means of an offer of monetary prizes, to get up a small race-meeting, the races being ridden over a quarter mile course, barebacked, go-as-you-please. The following is a list of winners: 1st Race. *For Bucks*. Peter Bigplume—1, Two Guns—2, Dodging-a-Horse—3. 2nd Race. *For Squaws*. Mrs. Bigplume—1, Mrs. Starlight (nee Miss Mary One Spot)—2, Mrs. Foxtail—3.

The squaws ride barebacked, as well as their male relatives, but are sometimes tied on, by means of a long sash, which is passed like a girth round the pony and over the knees of these female Mazeppas.

The third race, for boys, is marred by an accident, caused by one of the jockeys parting company with his steed at (what the Private Secretary is facetiously pleased to term) Tattenham Corner, the runaway pony subsequently knocking down an Indian who makes a gallant attempt to stop it.

This unfortunate man being badly cut about the head and losing a quantity of blood, a great commotion arises among the squaws, who commence at once to weep and howl in a most painful and unnecessary manner.

Indians have an intense dislike to physical suffering of any kind and are apt to make a great fuss over a very small accident. Fortunately, on this occasion, a doctor is present to attend to the injured man; he is soon able to pronounce that no bones are broken and that the wound is nothing worse than an external abrasion of the cuticle, which though painful and somewhat serious, can be relieved to a very great extent by a little offering of coin of the realm. A paper bandage, composed of dollar notes, has a wonderfully soothing effect on the patient, and, after a few similar applications, he promises to recover rapidly.

In the evening we return to Calgary, and, on the way home, Commissioner Perry has a slight disagreement with the horse he is riding; a disagreement which might have ended in per-

sonal violence but for the Commissioner's tact in stepping
lightly off the animal's back while in a state of rapid transit.
The argument is continued from terra firma, but the impatient
steed, not having any suitable logic at his command, refuses to
wait for the remainder of the Major's "winged words" and
moves off at a rapid rate towards the horizon. His desertion is
intercepted by a batch of mounted policemen specially de-
spatched for his arrest, after which the quarrel is apparently
made up and he and his master proceed upon their journey in
a state of amicable mutual attachment.

At Calgary Their Excellencies hold a Reception at the Opera
House and an address of welcome is presented by the Mayor
and Aldermen.

On Tuesday (September 19th) we are given a day's prairie
chicken shooting on the ground of the Indian Reserve, a party
of about six guns getting a bag of thirty-six brace, much of
which falls to Her Excellency's unerring birding-iron.

The weather is glorious, and, in the distance, the Rockies
stand out white and clear in the splendid sunshine of a typical
North Western day.

It is perhaps ungrateful to criticise, and no doubt this day's
shooting cannot be taken as a true specimen of sport in Western Canada; certainly, to the captious English eye, the method
of approaching the birds is a curious one.

The party of sportsmen advance in the following order across
the prairie. First Their Excellencies and the other guns, in a long
line, in skirmishing order, no "dressing" of any kind being kept,
and no proper intervals between the guns attempted; next
comes the cavalry, composed of mounted policemen in scarlet
and brown jackets, who follow a few yards behind the guns.
The order of advance is completed by the artillery and transport, consisting of a four-horsed police waggon and two other
carts, which are driven slowly behind the shooters, and occasionally, in the excess of their zeal, advance beyond the firing
line itself.

The birds are then complained of on account of their wild-
ness, a condition which can hardly be avoided in the face of
such a triumphal procession as this. The dogs, four setters of
undoubted pedigree, are so alarmed by this scene of revelry

that they refuse to work, a state of things which cannot be wondered at, but which is extremely detrimental to any hopes or prospects of a big bag. They range wildly some miles ahead of the guns and put up all the birds on sight. Whether it is that their owners do not consider this behaviour extraordinary, that they cannot recollect the names of their dogs, or are unable to whistle, the fact remains that no attempt is made to diminish their zeal and the day's shooting proceeds in an aimless way, with comparatively little sport and positively no system.

Fortunately the weather is so superb and the party is so delightful and so intent on happiness, that it is a pleasure to be out of doors and in such charming society. The birds too are plentiful enough to counteract any attempts made by the ingenuity of man to diminish the size of the possible bag.

In the afternoon the guns are so jaded that they are forced to follow the dogs in carriages, dismounting at every "point," climbing back into their conveyances each time the light-hearted setter has discovered, with a look of pained surprise which custom cannot stale, that the object of his attention is merely a lark or gopher, and refreshing themselves copiously, and at frequent intervals, from the supply of liquid conveniently carried in the transport waggons.

"C'est magnifique, mais ce n'est pas le sport!" says the Comptroller, whose French is as fearless as it is above reproach.

It is perhaps a pity that a brass band, which would assuredly be more in keeping with the character of the day's sport, is not added, to complete the idea and give a general tone and finish to the outfit.

It would be curious indeed, if not shocking to a sensitive nature, to listen to the remarks of some old-fashioned Scotch game-keeper whose fate it was to witness a combined frontal attack of this kind made upon his moor; certainly no self-respecting Scotch grouse would remain in the same country to await the approach of such a tumultously alarming cavalcade as ours.

Leaving Calgary on the night of the 18th we arrive the next morning at Edmonton, Alberta, where another day of sunshine and heat waits us.

After the presentation of a civic address, in the grounds of the public school of the city, followed by a visit to the hospital, we ride nine miles out to the Mission of St. Albert, where the residents are awaiting our arrival.

The settlement of St. Albert is principally the work of Father Lacombe, a very well-known and justly popular French Canadian priest; is chiefly populated by colonists of his own nationality, and is in a most flourishing and prosperous condition.

More addresses are presented, and, after luncheon, which owing to its being a fast day, consists entirely of poached eggs and milk, a charming little performance is given by the children of the affiliated convent, and we leave St. Albert at about four P.M.

On the way home Her Excellency stops at the south bank of the Saskatchewan River, for the purpose of christening a new gold dredge belonging to the Saskatchewan Gold Proprietary Company, a ceremony which she performs with great success.

The bed of this river contains a vast quantity of gold, which can be obtained by a process similar to that employed in the placer mines of the Yukon.

The newly christened dredge, now proudly bearing the name of "The Minto," is capable of excavating an area of three thousand cubic yards per day from the soil of the river bottom. As, according to the statements of the sanguine manager, each yard is worth from twenty to twenty-five cents, and, as the actual working expenses only amount to about eight cents per yard, it is entirely probable that a brilliant future awaits the efforts of this Company.

The Comptroller is not to be moved by these promises of untold treasure and declares that he has no intention of becoming a shareholder; it seems wrong, he says, to make money so easily as all that; wrong—and risky!

This is perhaps one of our hardest working days, during eight consecutive hours of which we have been in the saddle, or walking round various places of interest, being shown things we didn't want to see. The fact that His Excellency has himself been called upon to make eight different replies to eight distinct addresses, at various times of the day, enables him to retire to rest with a conscience comfortably soothed with the knowledge of so much duty satisfactorily accomplished.

The country round Edmonton is rolling bush; the land, when cleared, exposes a rich fertile soil, in every way suitable for the growing of grain and the production of fruit, and offering a splendid field for the agriculturally-minded colonist.

Our last day in this district opens as brilliantly as ever, and we are tempted to try our luck once more in pursuit of the wily "chicken." After a short and pleasant day's sport we return with sixteen and a half brace of birds, two ducks and a partridge. The bag would have been larger but for the number of chickens which the Comptroller shot, himself observed to fall, and never could discover!

The Canadian partridge possesses the characteristics, or, at any rate, has acquired the proclivities and habits, of the ordinary domesticated cat. On the approach of a dog, it does not fly away, after the manner of its English confrere, but merely runs up a tree, where it sits and smiles benignly at its pursuer from a lofty branch, and is apparently satisfied at being out of reach of its natural enemy, who is reduced to barking hoarsely and indignantly on the ground below. When the owner of the dog appears on the scene, he will either, if out for sport, push the unfortunate bird off the tree and shoot it on the wing, or, if his intentions are strictly culinary, will raise his gun, close the left eye with great deliberation and proceed to blow the wretched partridge up, on its temporary perch, at a range of about three yards.

We return to Calgary on the 21st, Their Excellencies having made various engagements to visit the hospitals and convents of that city.

At all the bigger convents of the Dominion the receptions held on the occasion of a visit from distinguished persons are invariably similar; the chief feature of the entertainment being a short musical performance given by the convent children. Each of these institutions appears to possess a tame poet, who is able, at a moment's notice, to produce any amount of doggerel of a well-meaning but unrhythmical order, suitable for any occasion. Poetic license is made free use of by these bards and the Private Secretary suggests that he himself might perhaps hope to compete with some success, if he were allowed to take out a *dog*-gerel license! (It is sad to see a young man giving way to the temptations of the private buffoon and perpetrating this type of joke; but the Private Secretary was always a wilful lad.)

In every important convent there is a large reception-room, in which stand eight or more pianos, and, at each of these instruments, 3 little girls, becomingly attired in clean white frocks, are usually seated, with the praiseworthy intention of industriously and laboriously producing a large number of notes in a very short space of time.

The favorite tune, usually adopted on these occasions, is an uninteresting march, illuminated by brilliant runs which lead nowhere, and punctuated by heavy reiterated chords, each of which promises to be final and fails to carry out its promise.

The twenty-four children at the eight pianos perform the allotted piece with commendable consonance, painstaking precision and synchronism sufficient for the purpose; but the character of the composition and the collocation of instruments do not lend themselves to the production of any depth of feeling, lightness of touch or charm of tone.

The advantage of this system of combined musical education is hard to discover. But few families possess a sufficiency of infant prodigies suitable for a single trio upon the piano; still fewer can, or even care to, provide more than one piano per room; and one may be permitted to conjecture that no self-respecting pater-familias would be willing to bear, for any length of time, with the results produced by a number of these congested instruments.

On Saturday (September 22nd) we reach Gleichen (pronounced "Gleesham" by the natives), a short run from Calgary, for the purpose of visiting the large Blackfoot Reserve, situated in the neighbourhood.

In the morning the whole party, with the exception of the Aide-de-Camp, who is confined to his bed by an affection of the leg, rides and drives out to the Reserve, where the Blackfeet turn out in great force, and where the usual pow-wow and subsequent dances take place.

It is a matter of some difficulty to determine who exactly is the head chief of this tribe. The honours of the occasion are done by White Pup, but, at the pow-wow, he takes a back seat, and leaves the prominent places to two others.

The great chief, Crow Foot, now deceased, and whose widow is still the elderly but fashionable leader of the Reserve society, and, unlike other squaws, is admitted, at the pow-wow, into the sacred circle of the chiefs, nominated as his successor to the chieftainship a certain man named Iron Shield.

The Government, however, appeared to have ignored this wish of his, or, at any rate, neglected to carry it out, and subject to the election of the people, appointed Running Rabbit as head chief.

This nomination presently caused some discontent, and it was finally decided that Iron Shield and Running Rabbit should rule alternately, each being chief for a year in turn.

Among the minor chiefs present we notice Medicine Child, Weasel Calf, Yellow Horse, the latter in all the panoply of his war-paint, with his squaw and papoose, elegantly arrayed in the canary colours of his house, forming a gay and brilliant picture; Little Axe, Big Road, Running Marten, Calf Child, an old head warrior, Eagle Ribs, and many others bearing similarly attractive appellations.

Some have donned the gaudy head-dresses and feathers so dearly loved by the race; others content themselves with a coating of paint and a breech cloth; while the interest attached to the personality of many is enhanced by the presence of numerous scars with which their bodies are liberally scored, and which serve as memories of the bygone scenes of bloodshed in which they took part, in those happy days when they were allowed to go on the war-path and fight their neighbours whenever they felt inclined for a little gentle exercise.

While this entertainment is going on here, another performance of a somewhat different nature is being given at Gleichen, where the unfortunate Aide-de-Camp has placed himself unreservedly in the hands of the local practitioner. An operation being thought necessary, the worthy doctor, without the aid of chloroform, cocaine or anaesthetic of any sort, and with a single-edged and not over keen knife, which he sharpens upon his boot and with which he admits to never having used upon any material other than tobacco, makes two cross cuts, over an inch in length and half as deep, in that portion of the patient's leg which is already so tender that to touch it with the finger is agony.

The picture does not bear to be further dwelt upon, but the intelligent mind can easily comprehend the acme of human suffering attached to this very unnecessarily barbarous treatment.

Leaving Gleichen this evening we arrive, on Sunday, at Regina, where Their Excellencies are to be the guests of the Lieutenant Governor and Madame Forget.

The next day is spent in visiting public institutions, receiving addresses and holding a Reception in this doleful capital of the North West Territories, a city which is now made the more unalluring by a continued downpour of rain which falls without cessation all day long.

On closer inspection Regina appears, if possible, an even less desirable place of residence than it seemed at first sight surrounded by dry, barren prairie, as far as the eye can reach; with neither shade from sunshine nor shelter from rain; it must appear, to the eye of the weary immigrant, a very inferno of flat unprofitable dullness.

Regina is the headquarters of the North West Mounted Police; here do the recruits undergo their preliminary course, and, that they can contrive to live through their stay here without suffering from feelings of mutiny or incipient idiocy says much for the prestige of the Corps and the physique of the men enlisted.

Occupation there is none, and even the harmless pastime of riding across the plains is put a stop to by the many concealed cracks and fissures by which the ground is broken up and into which the unwary cavalier may fall. Horsemen are forced to stick closely to the tracks or trails, which, one may say in parenthesis, lead nowhere.

This evening the party leaves Regina for Saskatoon, which they reach the next morning at an early hour, in a storm of wind and snow, Their Excellencies receiving an address here and departing soon afterwards.

Prince Albert is reached on the evening of September 25th and it is Their Excellencies' intention to spend two days here, previous to starting on their camping expedition to Qu'Appelle.

Meanwhile the Aide-de-Camp is left sadly behind at Regina, with the prospect of a lonely journey back to Ottawa on the morrow.[1] His place in the Vice-Regal party is adequately filled by Lady Violet Elliot, the sunshine of whose smile and the glitter of whose curls more than make up for the jaded buffooneries of the Aide-de-Camp, whose humour is, according to the Comptroller, "occasionally amusing, frequently trying, and generally coarse."

When last seen the patient is lying in his little cot in the train, smoking his twenty-seventh cigarette, and saying rude, unkind things about the house flies, which, in their present prehibernal state of somnolency, are as troublesome as they are numerous. They walk about upon his food, they climb laboriously over his face or perch flippantly on his nose; they come between him and his meals, and they have made his bed their particular dressing-room.

No other living thing, save perhaps a woman and a cat, spends so much time over its toilette as a house-fly.

She will stand for hours on her four hind legs, while she

[1] In his diary (September 19th, 1900) Lord Minto tells of the pocket knife operation Graham had for a carbuncle when they were at Gleishen. He says Graham suffered "perfect agonies" and the doctor in Regina would not hear of him going to Batoche and the ensuing march.

washes her hands with invisible soap, a proceeding in the course of which she seems to pay particular attention to her wrists. Then she will suddenly raise her arms in the air and brush her hair well down over her eyes several times, with a vigour which threatens to loosen her head and dislocate her neck. After this she stands on her front legs and wipes her back feet together violently for some time.

Either a fly's hands and feet become inordinately sticky as she walks about through the world, and her head requires an undue amount of combing and scratching, or else it is mere vanity that induces her to spend the best hours of a short life in such unnecessary efforts after the amelioration of her personal appearance.

The rest of the party are now at Prince Albert, a straggling township formed of three separate settlements, on the Saskatchewan River, which flows like a silver thread among the golden expanse of birch-clad scenery, and in its sinuous course bears a dim resemblance to the Yukon.

The day (September 26th) is spent in visits to three schools, a hospital and the Indian Mission, Emanuel College. The weather is appalling; three inches of snow cover the ground wherever it is not already covered with six inches of mud and the cold is intense.

In the evening Their Excellencies attend an amateur theatrical performance given by the ladies of Prince Albert. The play, entitled *Freezing a Mother-in-Law*, a name which is singularly suitable to the prevailing climatic conditions, proceeds satisfactorily and earns the measure of success to which such praiseworthy representations inevitably attain.

After this entertainment the party proceeds to the train, leaving during the night for Duck Lake, some thirty-eight miles away, where the morning of September 27th dawns warm and bright.

At Duck Lake the first blood was shed in the North West Rebellion of 1885 where His Excellency served, as Lord Melgund, with the troops of the Dominion.

Today the morning is given up to shooting. The party takes up a suitable position on the watertank of the engine, which patrols the line and from which point of vantage a bag of nine-

teen brace of chickens is obtained, Her Excellency especially distinguished herself by shooting nine brace to her own gun.

The next morning all go out once more on the engine, but without much success, and in the afternoon the start to Batoche is made on horseback, the party being accompanied by Captain Gilpin Brown and an escort of the North West Mounted Police.

On the way a short visit is paid to Father Paquet's Industrial School, a flourishing and seemingly well-conducted seminary, whose garden is a source of great satisfaction to the cheery old priest, and where the Indian boys and girls, to the number of one hundred, present an address to His Excellency and sing the usual hymns of welcome.

Batoche is reached towards evening, and, after crossing the ferry, the standing camp is pitched in time to afford shelter from a heavy thunderstorm which descends at about seven-thirty P.M. in a downpour of drenching rain.

The waggon containing the servants and some of the baggage upsets en route and the former arrive in camp at a very late hour, wet through and physically damaged in various places, but still retaining their invariable good spirits.

The first night in camp is bitterly cold, the water in the basins is frozen hard, and Her Excellency and Eileen, who are sharing a tent, are unable to get to sleep until nearly six A.M. next morning. They are much irritated at being wakened up an hour later by His Excellency, who breaks into their slumbers in the most lighthearted of moods and the scantiest of costumes for the purpose of lighting their stove.

The Comptroller, Commissioner Perry, and the Private Secretary pass a merry night in another tent, where they are occasionally visited by chipmunks and other rodents, which seem to have taken a fancy to the Private Secretary's boots, which they regard as an article of diet sent down for their special consumption by a merciful Providence who has not entirely forgotten the good old days of manna.

The morning is fine but cold and Their Excellencies spend some hours exploring Batoche. They visit the old Church and inspect the site of the camp occupied by General Middleton's troops in 1885, which can still be recognized and is surrounded by the remains of the old rifle pits used by the attacking rebels. The afternoon is given up to sport, the party getting a bag of

thirteen brace of chicken and one snipe, the latter by a magnificent shot of His Excellency.

On Sunday the weather grows warmer, and after breakfast the party rides out along the south bank of the Saskatchewan river, a distance of eighteen miles, to Fish Creek. His Excellency here recognizes the old battlefield and is much interested at revisiting the various positions of the troops, and particularly the point of vantage occupied by "Gat" Howard's quick-firing gun, which was one of the chief features of the locality on the occasion of his last visit to Batoche.

A colony of Galicians is settled in this neighbourhood, and, though they find it hard work to make a living on the products of the soil, the smallness of their means seems to have little effect on the picturesqueness of their appearance. They live in wooden shanties consisting of two sloping tent-shaped walls and possess no means of ventilation or light save by the single door in the front end of these peculiar lean-tos.

Galician men, clad in sheepskin coats, which they wear with the wool turned inside and which are held in with roughly worked native belts; Galician women, picturesquely accoutred in bright petticoats and scarves, their heads covered with brilliant green and pink handkerchiefs, are everywhere to be met with.

In the afternoon the return journey to Batoche is made, and, after a few anecdotes from the Comptroller, a little useful information on current topics from the Private Secretary, and much general conversation round the camp fire, a warm drink is indulged in and shelter of the blankets is sought at ten-thirty P.M.

On October 1st the party returns to Duck Lake, where Lady Minto, the children and the Comptroller take the train for Winnipeg. His Excellency, the Commissioner, Captain Brown, and the Private Secretary ride back to Batoche shortly afterwards and spend a third night in the standing camp.

Her Excellency's journey is broken at Qu'Appelle, where the special train collides with a trolley on the line and very nearly destroys a batch of workmen who were punting themselves along the track on this conveyance, and at Brandon where a drive round the Experimental Farm and a visit to the school is followed by luncheon with the popular Senator Kirchhoffer, better known under the title of Lord Burleigh of Brandon.

Winnipeg is reached on October 5th, and the hospitable Lieutenant Governor once more puts his house at the disposal of the Vice-Regal party. The chief feature of the stay at the capital of Manitoba is a Children's Fancy Dress Ball, given at Government House, at which Eileen appears as Lady Jane Grey, in the same dress worn by Her Excellency at the Devonshire House Ball of 1898, and Ruby as the Duchess of Devonshire in a most becoming Gainsborough hat. Vi, who has a soul above such frivolities as dancing, looks charming in powder, and wears the costume in which she won all hearts at the famous and oft-repeated dramatic performance of *The Princess and the Pauper,* when she appeared with such success at Ottawa in the spring of this year.

The ball is altogether a most successful one; a small boy as Kruger, two others as Mark Anthony and Coriolanus, a baby of two years old as a maple leaf, and a bewitching little girl in an Empire frock belonging to her grandmother, coming in for special commendation.

The next day Her Excellency visits the Deaf and Dumb Asylum, where the extraordinarily successful results of the wonderful system of teaching in vogue at this institution are clearly demonstrated; and, after lunch, the school children of Winnipeg give a most excellent performance of combined drill and singing at the Auditorium.

Her Excellency and the children return to Ottawa on October 6th in the car "Earnscliffe" and arrive at the Capital two days later, to the great joy of the Aide-de-Camp, who is waiting with outstretched arms to welcome them back to Government House. The Comptroller leaves Winnipeg on the following day for Brandon, for the purpose of rejoining the remainder of the party and sharing the pleasures of their sporting expedition.

Of the doings of His Excellency and party, whom we last heard of at Batoche, it is almost impossible to give any detailed narrative. Some account, however, of their famous ride to Qu'Appelle and of their duck shooting with Senator Kirchoffer may be gathered from the fragmentary notes made by the Private Secretary on his shirt-cuffs during his travels, notes which were rescued from the rapacious maw of the Ottawa Electric Laundry before the whole force of their descriptive beauty could be effaced forever.

The following extracts from the Private Secretary's log may be of sufficient interest to justify quotation:

October 2nd
His Excellency, Commissioner Perry, Captain Brown, twenty-three policemen, forty-three horses, five four-horsed waggons, and one two-horsed rig, the latter containing my flask, started this morning at nine-thirty A.M. from Batoche. Made twenty-two miles before lunch which was drunk in a snowstorm at a ranch called Batoche's. During lunch we saw no chicken. After lunch I saw several wild swans and they refused to go away.
Reached Vermilion Lake at teatime. Had dinner at eight-thirty P.M. Excellent dinner in a snowstorm followed by bed. N.B. I rode all day and felt no ill effects save a slight irritation at base of spine caused by sudden change of climate.
October 3rd
Warm and wet. Rode thirty-five miles to an old telegraph hut near

Humboldt where we camped. Wood on the prairie getting scarce but my flask still holds out.

October 4th

Wet and stormy. Rode twenty-six miles before lunch, which meal was drunk at the "Lake of the two Hills." Another eight miles after lunch. Dinner on salt plains. No wood for burning, except what we carried. No whisky ditto. N.B. wonderfully thirsty country this.

October 5th

Left six horses and waggon (not the two-horsed rig) behind to lighten loads. Trails very heavy. Lunched in snowstorm and arrived at Touchwood five-thirty P.M. Waggon with bedding and provisions broke axle and did not turn up till eight P.M. Had tea in house of Indian Agent. Had dinner an hour afterwards. Wanted to have supper but found that everyone had turned in.

October 6th

Breakfast in three inches of snow. The going is very bad. Started at eight-thirty A.M. with only personal luggage, escort of six men and two four-horsed teams. All the rest had to be left at Kutewa (Touchwood). Arrived at Mr. White's ranch, after ride of forty miles, at five P.M. Horses completely tired out. Found two-horsed light rubber-tyred trap waiting to drive His Excellency in to Qu'Appelle. His Excellency much bored by this, as he wished to ride the whole way. Arrived at Qu'Appelle with only six policemen and two waggons, the remains of our escort of twenty-three and our six waggons. How are the mighty fallen! At Fort Qu'Appelle we were received by Mr. Macdonald, one of the oldest Hudson's Bay men in the country, who came out here in 1854, and is one of the few "Chief Factors" left. He had entertained His Excellency in 1885, and was delighted to extend a similar hospitality to the Governor General again.

October 7th

After a visit to Hudson's Bay store rode in to Qu'Appelle station. Arrived in time for lunch at which champagne took a prominent place in the menu. Bade farewell to Perry and Brown who left after dinner for the West.

October 8th

Woke at Poplar Point. How did I get here? Ah, the train, of course. Found Senator Kirchhoffer and the Comptroller waiting for us. Drove out fourteen miles to a marsh on Lake Manitoba. Thence by canoe to the House on the Marsh, the Senator's shooting box. Got

twenty-eight ducks after dinner. Shack is not over-comfortable, consisting of one room in which everything except the actual cooking of
meals is done. Had to share a plank bed with the Comptroller, who is
unpleasantly angular. The Senator slept on floor, which was of fair
dimensions. Snoring proceeds all night, only interrupted by a ghostly
knocking at two A.M. General inclination to attribute this to spiritual
influence. Personally consider it the work of Providence.

October 9th
Breakfast five A.M. Total bag one hundred and eighty-four duck.

October 10th
Tea four A.M. Bag two hundred and sixty-five duck.

October 11th
Breakfast eleven A.M. Bag one hundred and thirty-nine duck. Left for
Poplar Point at noon and started on Imperial Limited for Ottawa at
nine-thirty P.M.

October 12th
On the train. Slept all day.

October 13th
Reached Ottawa eight-thirty P.M.

Here the Private Secretary's journal comes to a sudden close
and no more facts can be elicited from this trustworthy source;
from which it may be inferred that the tour of the Great North
West is at an end.

The tour is ended! The Imperial Limited glides slowly into
Ottawa, six hours behind time; the Guard of Honour presents
arms, the band executes the National Anthem, His Excellency
steps out of the car Victoria and greets the numerous officials
who have come to welcome him home, the travelling escort of
dragoons forms up and the Governor General of the Dominion drives off amid the plaudits of the assembled multitude.

The tour is ended! The Private Secretary leaps off the platform of the train with the agility of a monkey, if not with the
grace of a gazelle, and throws himself rapturously into the
arms of his expectant family. The Comptroller steps languidly
out upon the side-walk and allows eight of his latest conquests
of the female persuasion, who are anxiously awaiting his
arrival, to throw themselves into his arms, while he maintains
that customary attitude of imperturbable self-possession which

has always endowed him, in the eyes of his fellowmen, with the interest of inscrutability, and in the eyes of the ladies of his acquaintance, with the fascinating attraction of mystery.

Meanwhile the Aide-de-Camp, who has come down to the depot to meet the returning travellers, and who, with the consciousness of a general personal unpopularity with both sexes, knows that such welcomes are not for him, is wandering about the platform with his mouth full of baggage checks, trying, amid the discordant babel of ubiquitous hotel touts, to save the Vice-Regal baggage from the clutches of an unauthorized expressman.

Small wonder then that, as he watches the Private Secretary's proud and happy family gathering the prodigal to their bosom; as he sees the Comptroller's eight latest admirers all endeavouring to pat their hero simultaneously; the Aide-de-Camp should be surprised by the presence of a choking sensation at the throat, of a tear dimming the lustre of his shining eye. He realizes—alas!—that no bosoms pant for his return, and that nobody has ever had the slightest desire to pat him.

With a metallic laugh he turns away from a scene of simple childlike revelry which it is not for him to share, and, with the absent-mindedness born of patient and deliberate study, steps into the Comptroller's hired fly and drives in solitary grandeur to Government House.

The tour is ended! Three months of time, ten thousand miles of distance have been spent, accomplished, traversed, since that bright July day on which the party left Ottawa for the Arctic regions of the Klondyke; and now Ottawa looms once more into view, and the Capital of the Yukon fades away into the distance of the past.

From Dawson to Ottawa is a far cry indeed; yet taking into consideration the dates of the respective foundations of the mining camp and the Capital, a comparison between the two is distinctly unfavourable to the latter. The "City of sawdust and Civil Servants" stands still, while the settlement of saloons and spirits, of gold and gaiety, advances!

The roads of Dawson are open to criticism, certainly, and yet in Ottawa, where the virgin rock stands out with a certain rugged picturesqueness from the macadam of the principal

by-streets, the state of the thoroughfares is not altogether beyond reproach.

Dawson affords poor shelter to the traveller? Perhaps. The
hotel accommodation of Ottawa is avowedly inadequate to the
requirements of visitors.

Do you cavil at the amusements of the mining camp? Its
music halls are not above criticism certainly. Yet one may
venture to state that, during the last five years, not more
than a dozen second class and certainly less than half a
dozen first class theatrical performances have been presented
to Ottawa audiences, in the playhouses which it is their privilege to frequent, the mediocrity of whose productions is notorious.

The press of the Yukon is not particularly readable, the quality of its foreign news suffering chiefly from the result of being
almost entirely of home manufacture. It will nevertheless be
generally allowed that the daily journals of the Capital, with
their paucity of interesting intelligence and their wealth of de-
grading advertisements, are, in proportion to their circulation,
on a far lower level than the scrappy news-sheets of the mining
settlement.

It is of course ridiculous to make any serious comparison
between the two such extremes as the mushroom Arctic village
and the highly civilized Eastern City; one distinct advantage,
however, the former now holds over the Capital of the Dominion—Dawson has no Mayor and Corporation!

The tour is ended, and the writer of these pages looks back
with the dissatisfied eye of self-criticism at his attempted description of an experience which has been on the whole enjoyable, frequently most interesting and always unique.

His criticisms may be accused, and with justice, of being in
many cases founded upon the insular prejudices of the average
English mind; his judgments are too often based upon an ignorance of facts; his opinions biased by temporary local consid-
erations of personal comfort; his views qualified by the chronic
condition of his digestion.

The short time allotted to the visiting of each point of interest along the route must be responsible for many misstate-
ments; the lack of a talent for accurate perception and of any

adequate powers of literary expression must be reason enough for much in this journal that is dull and unprofitable; the state of mental fatigue resulting from the conditions involved in a period of perpetual travelling, wearing to the nerves and trying to the temper, must be the cause of many critical errors of taste and judgment. "I have never thought it easy to be just," says one who was probably the most broadminded and kindly of modern writers, "and daily find it harder than I thought."

In this journal there is no record of stirring deeds or gallant actions; no personal bravery is to be met with, save the courage daily displayed by the Comptroller in walking about on legs whose slimness is a matter of hourly trepidity to his friends and of personal gratification to himself.

No halo of romance sheds its brilliant light around these pages, save that glamour of mystery which naturally attaches itself to a Private Secretary who is ever endeavouring to forget that he was once in the Marines, and to behave as though he were unconscious of the presence of "a wife in every port."

No wit enlivens the dreary monotony of this narrative, save the occasional scintillations of the Aide-de-Camp whose sense of humour is a source of unfailing and shameless pride to himself as it is of surprise and trial to his relations.

This journal does not pretend to the attractions of a work of fiction, nor to the utility of a guide book. Its intention is to pose merely as an amateur description of primary impressions rather than as the vehicle for any deliberate opinions. Its one purpose is the simple narration of a pleasant personal experience, rather than the didactic statement of actual facts. It points no morals, draws no conclusions; and, if it possesses a single praiseworthy quality, that quality is Truth.

FINIS.

Harry Graham

1900.

Appendix A

Table of Approximate Distances and Dates*	Miles (Approximately)	Date	
		Depart	Arrive
Ottawa to Vancouver	2,790	July 19th	July 30th
Vancouver to Victoria	84	July 31st	July 31st
Victoria to Skagway	927	Aug. 4th	Aug. 10th
Skagway to White Horse	111	Aug. 10th	Aug. 10th
White Horse to Dawson City	452	Aug. 11th	Aug. 14th
Dawson to Victoria	1,490	Aug. 17th	Aug. 31st
Victoria to Vancouver	84	Sept. 5th	Sept. 5th
Vancouver to New Westminster	18	Sept. 6th	Sept. 6th
New Westminster to Glacier	415	Sept. 6th	Sept. 7th
Glacier House to Arrowhead	72	Sept. 9th	Sept. 9th
Arrowhead to Robson	124	Sept. 10th	Sept. 10th
Robson to Rossland	32	Sept. 10th	Sept. 10th
Rossland to Nelson	60	Sept. 12th	Sept. 12th
Nelson to Kootenay Landing	45	Sept. 12th	Sept. 13th
Kootenay Landing to Lethbridge	187	Sept. 13th	Sept. 13th
Lethbridge to Calgary	144	Sept. 15th	Sept. 17th
Calgary to Edmonton	190	Sept. 18th	Sept. 18th
Edmonton to Calgary	190	Sept. 21st	Sept. 21st
Calgary to Regina	483	Sept. 22nd	Sept. 23rd
Regina to Prince Albert	250	Sept. 24th	Sept. 25th
Prince Albert to Duck Lake	38	Sept. 27th	Sept. 28th
Duck Lake to Batoche	7	Sept. 28th	Sept. 28th
Batoche to Qu'Appelle	200	Oct. 2nd	Oct. 6th
Qu'Appelle to Poplar Point	284	Oct. 7th	Oct. 8th
Poplar Point to Ottawa	1,324	Oct. 11th	Oct. 13th
Total	10,001 miles	88 days	

*N.B. This does not include rides to Banff, Dawson, Edmonton, etc.

Appendix B

*List of Places Personally Visited by Their Excellencies
in the Course of the Tour*
(a) The Presentation of Addresses
(b) A Public Reception, Banquet or Ball

Alert Bay
Arrowhead
Banff
Bennett
Brandon
Calgary(a)(b)
Comox
Dawson(a)(b)
Duck Lake
Edmonton(a)
Esquimalt
Fish Creek
Glacier House
Gleichen
Keewatin
Lethbridge(a)
MacLeod
Magrath
Metlah Catlah
Nanaimo(a)

Nelson(a)(b)
New Westminster(a)
Okotoks
Poplar Point
Prince Albert(a)(b)
Qu'Appelle
Rat Portage
Regina(a)(b)
Revelstoke
Robson
Rossland(a)(b)
Saskatoon(a)
Selkirk
Skagway
Stirling(a)
Touchwood
Vancouver(a)(b)
Victoria(a)(b)
White Horse(a)
Winnipeg(a)(b)

Bibliography

Primary Sources

Minto Correspondence. The National Library of Scotland and the
   Public Archives of Canada.
Lord Minto's Scrapbook. The National Library of Scotland.
Lord Minto's Diary. The National Library of Scotland.
Lady Minto's Private Correspondence. The National Library of
   Scotland.
The Arthur Elliot Correspondence. Minto Papers, Public Archives
   of Canada.
London Newspapers 1900–1936. Newspaper Library of the British
   Museum, London.
Conversations with and letters from Mrs. Virginia Thesiger.

Secondary Sources

Asquith, Margot, Countess of Oxford and Asquith, ed. *Myself When
   Young—By Famous Women of Today*. London: Frederick Muller
   Ltd., 1938.
Barrymore, Ethel. *Memories: An Autobiography*. New York: Harper &
   Brothers, 1955.
Berton, Pierre. *Klondike*. Toronto: McClelland and Stewart, 1958.
Buchan, John. *Lord Minto: A Memoir*. London, Edinburgh and New
   York: Thomas Nelson and Sons, 1924.
Dafoe, John W. *Clifford Sifton in Relation to His Times*. Toronto: Mac-
   millan, 1931.
Hamilton, W.R. *The Yukon Story*. Vancouver: Mitchell Press Limited,
   1964.
Hubbard, R.H. *Rideau Hall*. Ottawa: Queen's Printer, 1967.
Morgan, Murray. *One Man's Gold Rush*. Photographs by E.A. Hegg.
   Seattle and London: University of Washington Press, 1967.

176   "New Parliament Buildings, Victoria, B.C." Government of British
Columbia leaflet. Provincial Archives of British Columbia.

Pope, Joseph, C.M.G. Undersecretary of State. *The Royal Tour in
Canada, 1901.* Ottawa: S.E. Dawson, Printer to the King's Most
Excellent Majesty, 1903.

Secretan, J.H.E., C.E. of Ottawa. *To Klondyke and Back: A Journey
Down the Yukon from its Source to its Mouth.* London: Hurst and
Blackett, Limited, 1898.

Who Was Who. Vol. 3, 1929–1940, 2nd ed. London: Adam &
Charles Black.

Who's Who in the Theatre.

Geographical Sources

Akrigg, G.P.V., and Helen B. Akrigg. *1001 British Columbia Place Names*. Vancouver: Discovery Press, 1969.

Holmgren, Eric J., and Patricia M. Holmgren. *Over 2000 Place Names of Alberta*. Saskatoon: Western Producer Book Service, 1973.

Hunter, M.F., City Clerk of Victoria. Letter dated 12 July 1960, re: Leper's Island. Provincial Archives of British Columbia.

International Joint Commission on the Lake of the Woods Reference. *Final Report*. Washington, DC: Government Printing Office, 1917. Kenora Public Library.

Mardon, Ernest G. *Community Names of Alberta*. Lethbridge: University of Lethbridge, 1973.

Middleton, Lynn. *Place Names of the Pacific Northwest*. Victoria: Elldee Publishing Co., 1969.

Morris, Frank, and Willis R. Heath. *Marine Atlas*, Vol. 2, Port Hardy to Skagway. Seattle: PBI Co., 1971.

Russell, E.T., ed. *What's in a Name? Travelling through Saskatchewan*. Saskatoon: Western Producer Book Service, 1973.

Wagner, Henry R. *Cartography of the N.W. Coast of America to the year 1800* (Vol. II). Berkeley: University of California Press, 1937.

Walbran, Captain John T. *British Columbia Coast Names 1592–1906*. Vancouver: The Library's Press, reprinted 1971.

Maps

"The Province" Map of the Klondyke and the Canadian Yukon and Routes Thereto. Victoria and Vancouver: The Province Publishing Company, 1897. Reissued by the Public Archives of Canada.

"The Map of Maps" Alaska and British Columbia, showing the Yukon... . J.J. Millroy Map Publisher, 1898. Provincial Archives of British Columbia.

178

Map Shewing the Railways of Canada. Department of Railways and
Canals Canada, 31st December 1900. Public Archives of Canada.

"Map of Dominion of Canada." Engraved for *The Globe* 1900, 1903.
Public Archives of Canada.

Alaska Steamship Co. Map showing routes to the Gold Fields and
St. Michael. 1917. Public Archives of Canada.

Canadian Hydrographic Chart No. 3572, Pulteney Point to Scarlett
Point. 1967. Provincial Archives of British Columbia.

Maps of North Western, West Central and South Western British
Columbia. Department of Lands, Forests and Water Resources,
Province of British Columbia. Revised 1973, 1968 and 1972
respectively.

POEMS, STORIES, ESSAYS and
BIOGRAPHICAL WORKS
by HARRY GRAHAM

1899	*Ruthless Rhymes for Heartless Homes*	Edward Arnold, London
1902	*Ballads of the Boer War*	Grant Richards
	Baby's Baedeker	
1903	*Perverted Proverbs*	R.H. Russell, New York
1904	*Misrepresentative Men*	Gay and Bird, London
1905	*Fiscal Ballads*	Edward Arnold
	More Misrepresentative Men	Fox, Duffield & Co., New York
	Verse and Worse	Edward Arnold
1906	*A Song Garden for Children*	
	Misrepresentative Women	Edward Arnold
1907	*Familiar Faces*	Edward Arnold
1908	*A Group of Scottish Women*	Methuen & Co., London
1909	*Deportmental Ditties*	Mills & Boon
1910	*The Mother of Parliaments*	Methuen & Co., London
	The Bolster Book	Mills & Boon
1911	*Lord Bellinger*	Mills & Boon
	Canned Classics	Mills & Boon
1912	*The Perfect Gentleman*	Edward Arnold
1913	*The Motley Muse*	Edward Arnold
	Splendid Failures	Edward Arnold, London
1914	*The Complete Sportsman*	
1917	*Rhymes for Riper Years*	Mills & Boon
1919	*Biffin and His Circle*	Mills & Boon
1924	*The World We Laugh In*	Methuen & Co., London
1925	*The Last of the Biffins*	Methuen & Co., London
1926	*Strained Relations*	Methuen & Co., London
1928	*The World's Workers*	Methuen & Co., London

1930	*More Ruthless Rhymes*	
1930	*Adams Apples*	Methuen & Co., London
1933	*The Biffin Papers*	John Lane
1934	*Happy Families*	Jonathan Cape
1936	*The Private Life of Gregory Gorm*	Peter Davies
1919	Letters and Papers of Algernon Hyde Villiers with a Memoir by Harry Graham	

THEATRICAL WORKS
by HARRY GRAHAM

1901	*Little Miss Nobody*	Lyric Theatre
1914	*State Secrets*	Criterion Theatre
	The Cinema Star	Shaftesbury Theatre
1915	*Tina* (with Paul Rubens)	
1916	*Sybil* (English version and Lyrics)	
1917	*The Maid of the Mountains* (Lyrics)	
1919	*Our Peg* (Lyrics)	
1920	*A Southern Maid*	Daly's Theatre
	(with Dion Clayton Calthrop)	
	A Little Dutch Girl	Lyric Theatre
	(with Seymour Hicks)	
1921	*The Lady of the Rose* (Lyrics)	Daly's Theatre
1922	*Whirled into Happiness*	
	(from the Austrian; Lyrics)	
1923	*Head Over Heels* (Lyrics)	
	Madame Pompadour	Daly's Theatre
	(with Frederick Lonsdale)	
1924	*Our Nell* (Lyrics)	
	The Buried Cable, or Dirty Work	
	at the Crossroads (one act)	
	Toni (with Douglas Furber)	
	Orange Blossom (from the French)	
	Betty in Mayfair (Lyrics)	Adelphi
1925	*Cleopatra* (Lyrics)	
	Riquette (Lyrics)	
	The Grand Duchess (from the French)	
	Katja the Dancer (with Frederick	
	Lonsdale, from the German)	

	Clo-Clo (with Douglas Furber, from the German)	
1926	*Merely Molly* (Lyrics)	
	My Son John (Lyrics)	
	The Blue Mazurka (Lyrics)	
1928	*Lady Mary* (Lyrics)	
	By Candle Light (from the German)	Prince of Wales
1929	*Hunter's Moon* (from the Danish)	
1931	*The Good Companions* (Lyrics)	
	Lady in Waiting (adapted)	
	White Horse Inn	London Coliseum
	(English book and Lyrics)	
	The Land of Smiles	
	(English version and Lyrics)	
	Viktoria and Her Hussar	Palace Theatre
	(English version and Lyrics)	
1932	*Casanova* (adapted)	
	Rise and Shine	
	Roulette (adapted)	
	Doctors Orders (adapted)